20 YEARS OF J.C.

The MAN, *The* LEGEND, *The* LAWSUIT!

BY *J C Corcoran*

★★★ With a Foreword by Eric Mink ★★★

Library of Congress Control Number: 2004111507

ISBN: 1-891442-29-5

Virginia Publishing Co.
PO Box 4538
St. Louis, MO 63108
www.stl-books.com

Dedicated to

Nancy Kromm...

the original "transistor sister"

who made sure I didn't get run over,

who introduced me to WLS,

who sat me down in front of the TV on

February 9, 1964,

and who's been a terrific aunt

to Addison and Whitney.

★★★ Foreword by Eric Mink ★★★

So you're thinking: a *second* book by J.C. Corcoran? One wasn't enough?

Spare me the sarcasm and the snobbery.

Yes, Corcoran is a radio personality, performer and craftsman by trade, not a writer. Yet thousands of people in the St. Louis region found his first book — with a title even more cumbersome than this one's — worthy of their time, their attention and their $15.95. The memoir of places he'd worked, people he'd met and battles he'd fought turned an awful lot of listeners into readers, no mean feat in our age of short attention spans and visual obsessiveness.

This new book is less linear. It's part sequel, part journal, part media criticism/rant, part braggadocio, part silliness and (much to my surprise) part confessional — with no attempt to hide the substantial ego and the heart of the complicated person who wrote it.

Like the previous book, "20 Years..." immerses itself in the world according to Corcoran. Chapter One opens with the first of several running logs, starting with an alarm clock and ending with the sign-off of that day's show. The hours spent on the air, he says, are "the best part of the day."

Translation: The guy's a ham; he loves performing.

Subsequent chapters flash back to the collapse of his career in the winter of 2001-2002, its recovery the next fall and the steady climb of his new show at KIHT-FM to first place. If you sense a certain I-told-you-so smugness in this narrative, it's not your imagination.

Corcoran's previous book lamented, justifiably, the rise of mega-radio, and he briefly returns to the subject here, offering a performer's-eye perspective on the consolidation of station ownership in ever fewer giant media companies. The federal government — now obsessed with broadcast naughtiness — may no longer regard this practice as anti-competitive, but Corcoran makes a persuasive case that it's anti-creative.

His real target of opportunity this time, though, is local television news, and having spent several years on the inside as a regular contributor, he's well acquainted with the medium's soft underbelly.

Oddly enough, I've sometimes chided Corcoran on the air and off for his seeming lack of interest in network entertainment programming; that is, the shows most Americans actually see. For example, just getting him to watch more than an isolated episode of "Seinfeld" — it was only the paradigmatic comedy of the 1990s — was like pulling teeth.

This book reveals why it's been such a struggle: it turns out Corcoran has been using his multiple video recording devices for years to track local news broadcasts. In the process, he has amassed a damning library of missteps that he happily catalogues in great detail herein. Kind of warms my heart.

Toward the end of the book, Corcoran offers a chapter of lists of things that, well, he decided to arrange in lists. He's convinced that fans will enjoy them. To be honest, they leave me cold, but then he and I argue about some of this stuff all the time. Harry Chapin's "Taxi" is a top-20 favorite song? Please.

On the other hand, America is long overdue for an updating of the National Jerk Test concept pioneered by the late Steve Allen, and Corcoran's is a beaut. Who knew he had such strong opinions about human behavior?

My favorite part of the book, though, turns out to be something of an afterthought, a chapter that tries to jam in information that doesn't really fit anywhere else. Corcoran's literary device for this is an interview with himself, an exercise with a sizable self-indulgence quotient.

That said, the format also allows him to venture into some sensitive areas and to let down — to some degree, anyway — his usually formidable self-defenses.

Regular listeners, for example, have heard him talk about his Catholic upbringing and schooling in Chicago, but he speaks here much more expansively about that and about religion in general.

More revealing still are some reflective personal comments about the emotionally wrenching effects of his divorce and the missteps he made in its aftermath.

In the end, the ultimate truth about J.C. Corcoran becomes all too apparent.

Inside the body of this driven radio personality — bad back, bum foot and all — there's a TV weatherman crying to get out.

Eric Mink

October 2004

Introduction

Everything I ever needed to know about St. Louis I learned by writing a book.

In December of 2000 *Real Life Stories of JC and The Breakfast Club or Twenty Minutes in the Dark with Madonna* was met with surprisingly good reviews. I use the word "surprisingly" since a significant chunk of the book's content dealt with my verifiable belief that St. Louis hasn't always gotten a fair representation of what I've been trying to do on radio and television over the past 20 years. The book was written for fans, for people with some degree of curiosity, and for that dwindling percentage of the population with an open mind.

It's been said that if a comedian is performing for a crowd of 500 people, and 499 of them are laughing, he'll sit at the bar after the show and stew about the one guy who wasn't. In a way I suppose that sums up the first four-fifths of my first 20 years in St. Louis. Largely due to the overwhelming one-on-one response I received during the book-signing blitz of 2000, I finally concluded that it makes little sense to drive myself crazy trying to win over the professional J.C. Corcoran haters and, instead, decided to focus on you misguided, poor souls who find value or, at least, entertainment in what I do on the air each day.

To the schmucks who will pick this work apart line by line in radio chat rooms on the Internet, call me a liar and an egomaniac, and dispute my account of the various events described here, have at it. Go nuts. I stopped caring about your type years ago.

No, siree. I haven't made everyone believers by any means. Each of our local TV stations has the unenviable task of trying to fill hours and hours of local news, discussion, and entertainment programming each day. Nevertheless, I was summarily ignored by the producers and hosts of every morning show, midday show, afternoon show, evening show, weekend show, and public affairs show on every local, commercial channel when contacted four years ago about interview availabilities.

I find this especially curious since even a former radio traffic reporter who recently pooped out a *calendar* managed to get invited on several stations to promote the thing.

I suppose, then, it shouldn't come as a surprise that I felt little compulsion to "hold back" in the chapter you'll be reading that deals with deficiencies, deception, and the general decomposition that's come to typify local television news these days.

Yes, "news." The first book centered primarily on the radio business and its impact on my life. That story can't be told twice, so I've chosen to cover some other things I think you'll find interesting or funny about this increasingly insane business. Without any question I can report that the most-popular segment of *Real Life Stories* was the chapter in which I presented a brief, thumbnail sketch of a few dozen of the major celebrities I've had the opportunity to interview over the years. This "behind-the-scenes" stuff is big business in entertainment these days, and I'll be taking you about as "behind-the-scenes" as you can get without actually being in the studio with us.

This book is different from the first in that I'll answer a lot of the questions I've repeatedly been asked over my 20 years here. And let me answer one right away. Yes. I do write these books myself. Some people go to a therapist. I talk on the radio and write books.

But before you start getting the silly idea I'm finally easing into some sort of middle-aged, well-adjusted stupor, help yourself to the chapter in which J.C. Corcoran, someone who's been complimented on his interviewing skills, gets a crack at firing off a series of pointed questions at...himself.

While I was very pleased with the success of the first book, I was disappointed it didn't result in further clearing the record of the ridiculous rumors that have plagued my career here. I really did believe the book would change a lot of things but, alas, it only succeeded on that level for those who actually read it. But we have three to four times as many people listening now than we did at the oldies station when *Real Life Stories* was published four years ago. With our return to the top spot in St. Louis morning radio comes a louder voice, a bigger stage, and more people hearing the message.

When I got into this business 30 years ago, I was surrounded by a bunch of creative, idealistic kids. In every way from wardrobe to political persuasion, radio people expressed their collective individuality. The occasional Republican was not only shunned but usually suspected of being a narc. Since so little attention was given to the FM band, we took the opportunity to stretch our creative freedom and, lo and behold, invented a brand of broadcasting that overtook the 50,000-watt, former behemoths on AM.

Now, all of broadcasting has become Clear Channelized, corporatized and homogenized. AM radio has reinvented itself as a right-wing mouthpiece, and, for the first time anyone can remember, people are being hired and even, in some cases, fired on the basis of political affiliation as opposed to talent. Sound scary? It gets worse.

There are new and numerous challenges the broadcasting world simply won't be able to dodge much longer without doing potential, long-term damage to its best interests. Leading the list of threats are MP3s, CDs, satellite radio, and even a new, Web-based service that mimics nearly 1,000 local radio stations (allowing users to hear a version of their favorite station with far fewer interruptions). Then there's good, old-fashioned corporate greed that can allow the sales arm of radio to steer a station's programming efforts under the guise of "the client wants it" or "we gotta pay the bills." I'll be making a strong case for the idea that the radio industry has itself to blame for a large number of the problems it's facing today.

Want more? Toss in federal intervention. It's responsible for the most significant development in broadcasting in decades, and you'll be reading about its chilling effect on what you hear on the air each day. You'd think radio would have learned from watching what's happened to television as its viewers have segued to pay cable and satellite right under its nose. I'll point out why the absence of anyone with any real influence at the top of the electronic media industry nationally — plus the fact there's no watchdog locally — is allowing shortsighted executives to sabotage their own business. I'm not criticizing individuals about mistakes. Lord knows I've made more than my share. This is about policy. The broadcasting business is going to hell in a handbag, but there are a few of us left who still care enough about it not to go down without a fight.

And wherever you find such large stakes, power and influence you'll find...lawyers. When I announced the name of this book would be *20 Years of J.C. The Man. The Legend. The Lawsuit*, more than one smart-aleck remarked, "Which *one*, J.C.?!?!" It's true that if I had all the money I've had to exhaust on legal fees over the past 20 years I could have purchased a home or two in one of those fancy West County neighborhoods I'm only allowed to visit now. Staying on the cutting edge and staying out of trouble can become a full-time job, you know.

Tina Fey, the incomparably funny and wise head writer of *Saturday Night Live*, once observed: "Tragedy plus time equals comedy. Comedy and sadness doesn't work. Comedy and anger works very well." Try and keep that in the back of your head as you read. It applies to so much of what I've chosen to talk about.

One thing that hasn't changed is that we, as on-air talent, are still at the mercy of the people who may or may not choose to give us the chance to do this job. What you see and hear and, perhaps more importantly, what you don't see and hear often can be decided by one guy, sometimes with personal reasons that aren't even rational.

While much of my public life in the past year was spent basking in the joy of our return to the number-one position on the St. Louis morning airwaves, my private life was much different. That joy was counterbalanced by a period of great personal challenge, reflection, introspection, and an eventual recognition that I am a work in progress. There is much therapeutic value in being around good people, hanging with good friends, or seeing a good movie. My daughter Addison is now eleven. And Whitney will be nine. They are the loves of my life. And, of course, the game of baseball continues to captivate me as it did when I was young and had hair.

This book was written between January and September of 2004 amid the hammering, pounding, and general disturbance you'd expect from a large construction team building an enormous addition onto the home of my neighbors to the north. During deadline week in late September my neighbors to the south commissioned a major excavation along the length of our adjoining property. If some of my words in this book seem harsh, it probably just means the giant, outdoor table saw was being used that day.

In the final chapter of *Real Life Stories* I lamented that my controversial image would certainly keep me from ever being considered for, say, the Lifetime Achievement Award. Sometime during the year that followed — when I wasn't looking — Karen Kelly, John-John Canavera, Brian

McKenna, and Eric Mink submitted my name for consideration. Either it was a helluva proposal or they caught the panel at a weak moment, but I was presented that very award in the spring of 2001.

There are occasions I have to remind myself there's still much to like about this business.

Enjoy!

J.C. Corcoran
September 2004

Chapter 1

"What a long, strange trip it's been."
"Truckin'"
Grateful Dead

We're playing hurt today.

The alarm on my nightstand goes off at 4:15 each morning. Another alarm is set for 4:20, but this one, a clock radio, is across the room on top of the television. If, for some reason, the first one doesn't get the job done, the second, set with the volume cranked as high as it will go, will not only do the trick, but will also bring me to the brink of a pre-stroke condition.

On this particular Monday morning, co-host and producer Laurie Mac and I are coming off hosting the Cinema St. Louis Oscar party at the Coronado Ballroom the night before. By the time the marathon telecast concludes and I drive home, wind down, peel off my rented tuxedo, and rip through the TiVo recording in a search for highlights to play on the show, it's close to 1 a.m.

Three hours and fifteen minutes later the first alarm sounds. But this is one of those mornings I'm saved by the deafening howl of that second clock radio.

I wonder. Would it really be such a bad thing to just end it all right here?

It's a quick hop downstairs to my home office where I review and download forty-seven pages of show business news, feature stories, celebrity birthdays, and oddities from around the world that we'll use on today's show while simultaneously speed-searching through the CBS overnight news for anything else decent. I look up at the clock and realize I'm already running late.

On most days I could probably ease the pressure on myself by simply getting up a few minutes earlier, but since I started this job almost 30 years ago my approach has always been to sleep until the last imaginable minute, then race like hell to get on the air on time.

Back upstairs in the shower, my mind races. I've been known to have some of my best ideas in the shower. Today, it occurs to me that I could do a joke that the nominees for Best Special Effects Make-Up were *Lord of the Rings, Master and Commander*, and Joan Rivers on the red carpet.

I grab the first clothes I see. About 20 minutes later I'll be walking into the station. I'll remember nothing about the drive in.

In two or three hours St. Louis will be abuzz with hordes of people rushing to work and jamming the highways. But at this hour the city is lifeless against its lighted signs and building tops.

As I walk down the long hallway to the office I share with Laurie Mac next to the kitchen, I can hear one of the five Emmis Broadcasting stations whispering out of the overhead speakers embedded in the ceiling. Our technicians have a system installed that changes the station each hour. Ours never seems to be playing.

It's just after 5 a.m.

Laurie is already at her desk.

"How are yeeeeuuuuwww?" she asks in her trademark southern drawl. (For some reason that drawl becomes much more prominent when she talks on the phone or when she expresses affection or interest.)

"Okay. What time do you think you finally got to sleep?" I ask.

Her response falls somewhere between a sigh and a groan. It's the furthest she'll drift from a near-100 percent state of pleasantness all week. *How does she do it?* I think to myself. *And how does she look so good at this hour?*

While I'm busy copying, printing, scribbling, and sticking Post-It Notes on everything in sight, as usual, Laurie silently slips out of the office and off to the other side of the complex, where our on-air studio is located. It's not unusual for us not to speak again until the microphones go on for the first time just after 6 a.m.

One of the audio clips from last night's Oscar telecast has to be transferred from digital audio tape to one of the two, specially designed portable computers that bounces back and forth from our office to the on-air studio each day. That will use up another precious five minutes.

It's 5:35 a.m.

I have time for just one more quick glance at my e-mail. Amidst the dozens of solicitations for Viagra, penis enlargement potions, and personal "invitations" from slutty Latino women, I spot one message that was actually sent by a listener. Someone has sent me an attachment containing a photo of a 375-pound dude wearing a t-shirt that reads, "I Beat Anorexia." This is good enough to make it on our office door along with a picture of a gravestone with the name reading "Kaput" and a photo of a very attractive, very large-chested woman wearing a tank top that reads, "I Wish These Were Brains."

There was a time when I answered every single e-mail I was sent. Like a lot of things in this world, e-mail was a great idea that got ruined by the same kind of people who seem to ruin everything that starts out good.

There's a bit more activity in the building than usual today. Our pal, KMOV's Jamie Allman, who moonlights as a morning talk show host on the station just down the hall, is beginning a week-long experiment. He'll be paired with Smash, who had recently been let go at KLOU not quite two years after replacing me.

Radio.

Apparently Jamie has convinced his television station to feature their first program together on KMOV's morning news. A mobile news truck with a towering, 30-foot-tall mast sits just outside our front door at the Union Station Powerhouse. Hundreds of feet of thick cable are strewn throughout the building, all ending up connected to a camera in the tiny 97.1 studio. I have just enough time to sneak up behind Smash and plant a disgusting, sloppy, wet kiss on the back of his freshly shaven head.

"Manski!" Smash has been calling me by that name since our days together, over 20 years ago, at DC 101 in Washington. Don't ask.

Last Friday's show featured a hilarious discussion with *St. Louis Post-Dispatch* feature writer Joe Holleman about unintentionally funny movies like Jennifer Lopez' bomb, *Enough*. It will serve as today's "Replay" segment that hits the air a few minutes before 6 a.m.

Now begins the transfer to the studio of two portable audio computers, notebooks, folders, CDs, stacks of notes, and cell phones, along with a bottle of caffeine-free Diet Coke and two oranges.

It's 5:45 a.m.

I'm not even close to being ready for this.

About this time I have my first daily encounter with Ray Collier, who works behind the scenes on everything from programming music to managing software programs on the stations' many computers. Ray wanders past my office on the way to the kitchen, where he'll invariably pluck the most high fat, high sodium, nutritionally bankrupt item he can find from the vending machine. When he passes the office again I'll complete the morning ritual of lobbing a comment his way questioning his heterosexuality. Ray returns an accusation so vile and so funny I have to wonder from what deep, dark recesses of his brain such a thought has been lurking all this time. We both completely crack up.

Laurie's been busy preparing the studio for the past 20 minutes. Traffic reporter and co-host Jennifer Sparks also slipped in somewhere along the way and is setting up in her corner of the studio. "Sparky," as we call her, looks like she just stepped out of the shower, void of any makeup, hair styling or extravagant wardrobing. She looks sensational. It occurs to me no two women in radio ever looked this good, especially this early in the morning.

In what I theorize as standard behavior at every radio station in America, the weekend air staff has left a trail of trash, old newspapers, twisted wires, and other debris for us to clean up and/or undo in order to make the place the least bit presentable. Imagine what a plastic can full of banana peels, Whopper remains, coffee grounds, and other unidentifiable matter — all allowed to ferment for just short of three days — smells like. Then remember it's not even 6 a.m.

The touch of a computer screen in the on-air studio disables the autopilot function that's kept the station running for the last six hours with music, promos and a few commercials. When "Gimme Shelter" by the Rolling Stones fades out, we'll officially begin another day of live programming.

It's 5:50 a.m.

Over the course of the next two minutes I'll:

• play a short comedy bit off one computer by former *Saturday Night Live* star Kevin Nealon about alarm clocks...

• touch a second computer screen to play a station I.D....

• touch the screen again to play "Happy to See You Again," the show's signature theme for the past 20 years...

• quickly change the page on the computer screen while cueing up today's "Replay" segment on a third computer...

It's 5:52 a.m.

I have about seven minutes to head back to the office on the other side of the building to retrieve some notes I've printed from our Marketing and Promotion department regarding some giveaways scheduled to begin today. Someone who may or may not be associated with KMOV's technical crew inquires about coffee. My plea of ignorance isn't a cop-out. Unbelievably, not one of the four people on our show touches the stuff. That, among other things, qualifies us as freaks in this business.

It's a minute after 6, and John Ulett arrives on the scene. You might think the man who will be delivering the news to thousands of people all morning might require more preparation, but this is how John works.

"HELLO, J.C. CO-CO-RON!!!!" John exclaims with one of his many deliberate mispronunciations of my name.

"Nice of you to join us today," I reply sarcastically while pointing to a clock that indicates his first newscast is seconds away.

An obscure, orchestrated version of the 70's pop hit "Dancing Queen," taken from the soundtrack of the even more-obscure film *Muriel's Wedding* (which starred Toni Collette and Rachel Griffiths) wafts in.

BLAAAAAAANG!!!

The station news theme hits the airwaves and another edition of *The Showgram* has begun. Our listeners are about to hear four hours of conversation, jokes, interviews, and stream-of-consciousness, every ounce of which is completely and totally spontaneous. No rehearsals. No scripts.

The second our first break concludes, U-Man rushes to the refrigerator in the station kitchen on the other side of the complex. There, he'll stow away a bizarre mixture of strawberries, mushrooms, cantaloupe, pineapple, olives, broccoli, kidney beans, cucumber slices, baby corn, raisins, cherries, hot peppers, grapes, and sunflower seeds he hand-prepares daily and eats out of a huge, terrarium-like container. John insists he has to eat this concoction every day or his heart will come to a complete stop.

I'll be too busy to sit, to go to the bathroom, or to do much of anything unrelated to the show for the next two-and-a-half hours. When John, Jen, and Laurie's participation ends just after 9 a.m., I'll briefly kick the automation system back on. That will play a cluster of commercials followed by, for the first time all morning, two songs back-to-back, or roughly the amount of time needed for a bathroom break and the consumption of those two oranges I've been eyeballing since 5:45 a.m.

Laurie heads back to the office to return calls, make calls, attend planning meetings, set up interviews, research on the Internet, answer e-mail, tutor our intern, and try to catch her breath. Sparks heads home. She has to be back at 2:30 for her afternoon shift, where she splits her time among not two, but three of our stations. U-Man darts thirty feet down the hall to begin his four-hour shift on KSHE.

During the negotiations that brought me to the station in September of 2002, I told Operations Manager Rick Balis I had two ideas for the nine o'clock hour in which we begin the transition to a more music-intensive presentation. The first was a daily collection of Beatles' songs and rarities I call "Fab Four." Today I'll sandwich an amazing version of "Beware of Darkness" by Eric Clapton from *The Concert for George Harrison* CD in between "Honey Don't" and "Glass Onion," followed by an alternate version of "Penny Lane" in which the trumpet solo we're used to hearing midway through the song is replaced by a musical interlude that sounds like something Burt Bacharach cooked up.

Several months after I'd gone back on the air at K-HITS, the programming department received the results of an extensive music research project which indicated, among other things, that the Beatles were experiencing an almost unprecedented spike in appeal. I remember that day, and I remember the "how-the-hell-did-you-know-that" look from programming that came with it.

The second idea for the nine o'clock hour was to feature a forgotten song lost somewhere in the annals of record history. Though "The Vault" is usually one of my most-enjoyable moments of the day, it seems like someone always comes into the studio with something they need to discuss just as I'm about to crank something like Joe Walsh's "Funk 49" on the studio speakers to within a half-degree of their recommended factory limitations.

I hate it when that happens.

It's 9:45 and market veteran "Radio Rich" Dalton saunters into the studio and lays a weathered stainless steel briefcase on the countertop. Whereas I need computers, cabinets, stacks and stacks of notes, and an entire office to store the material I use each day on the show, remarkably, Rich seems to have everything he needs to do a show either in his briefcase or in that giant noggin of his.

Though the studio looked like a college dorm room following a freshman mixer just over an hour ago, Rich is about to inherit a spotless workspace. It's the way I was brought up in the business.

In just the next few minutes I'll go from the best part of the day...to the worst.

It's 10 o'clock.

Chapter 2

"Nothing but blues and Elvis and somebody else's favorite song..."
"FM"
Steely Dan

Real Life Stories of J.C. and The Breakfast Club or Twenty Minutes in the Dark with Madonna was released in the fall of 2001.

At that time I was in the middle of my stint at KLOU, working the morning show with my best friend, Karen Kelly, and longtime sports personality Brian McKenna. I'd had serious doubts as to whether our act would work on an oldies station, but I went into it the way I go into anything, and that's all the way. As was the case when we flew in the face of all prevailing wisdom and achieved our great successes at KSD, we did not buy into the idea that our show content had to conform to the sort of nostalgia normally associated with a station that played older music.

To clarify, in the '80s virtually every classic rock station in America instructed its on-air personalities to focus on the events, history, concerts, and icons of the late '60s and '70s. The managers and consultants of these stations thought it was crucial to their effort, but I never bought into that. For one thing, I thought doing things that way would limit our potential for broad appeal. From 1987 to 1991 while at KSD, our show focused on the events of the day. Most of the industry thought we were crazy to be playing older Eric Clapton and Van Halen music while talking about Madonna's sex book and Dana Carvey's George Bush impression on *Saturday Night Live*. Of course, when our ratings exploded, the entire industry took note, and soon, classic rock morning shows all over the country realized they didn't have to turn on the microphone and only talk about a Springsteen concert they saw in 1978 or their first eight-track player.

But in accepting the offer from KLOU, that theory was being stretched a lot farther. Could we really still talk about current events on a station that played 35-year-old music and traditionally focused on nostalgia?

KLOU had spent over $300,000 on television commercials to promote our show when it launched earlier that year. But just a few weeks after we'd gone on, the station's antenna literally burned up. That meant we had no choice but to flip to the decrepit back-up system while a new antenna was ordered. We immediately got two big surprises. First, we were told the new system wouldn't arrive for several months. Second, that backup transmitter, which was only intended for emergencies, didn't even cover the St. Louis metropolitan area. One of our station managers reported he couldn't even pick up the station on his clock radio at his home in O'Fallon, Missouri.

It was déjà vu all over again.

As was the case at The River in the mid-'90s before they moved the station's transmitter from East Jesus to north St. Louis, thousands of potential listeners were unable to hear the station unless they were in cars. That meant we had little chance of building an audience. It also meant that $300,000 was, essentially, wasted.

Finally, more than five months after the main antenna blew, we were back at full power in October of 2001. We felt as though we were starting all over again. KLOU had broadcast rights to the defending world champion St. Louis Rams; we arranged for Marshall Faulk to be on our show each week; my book was ready to hit the stores; and things were on the move.

However, over the next few months the growth of the show's audience was less than meteoric. We'd taken over a tenth-place show, and everyone had expected big things from us. Privately, I wondered if the kind of show we did was conducive to the oldies format. Publicly, I kept plugging away. It paid off because the numbers started rolling in during the spring of 2002, when we jumped into a fifth-place tie. That was the good news. The bad news was that the station as a whole was lagging far behind.

KLOU's management had been begging the company for money to conduct a "music test" for quite some time. Finally, in the summer of 2002, that wish was granted, and the test was performed.

"What's a music test?" you ask.

Imagine an auditorium filled with a hundred people, each one carefully selected by a company whose job it is to scan the phone book and pick a representative sampling of men and women in several age groups, each paid $75 to $100 and, most importantly, fed well. Equally important, however, they've been told the exercise is being conducted by "an independent research company." That's necessary so as not to influence their responses in any way. It's also important for still another reason I'll get to in a moment.

The group is then subjected to several hours of music "hooks," or the most-repeated or prominent part of the song. For example, the "hook" in the song "Good Vibrations" by the Beach Boys is the part in which they sing:

"I'm pickin' up good vibrations.
She's givin' me excitations.
I'm pickin' up good vibrations..."

The hook in the song "I Saw Her Standing There," for example, is:

"Well, I'll never dance with another
Since I saw her standing there..."

After each hook, the respondents are instructed to rate the individual song on a scale of one to ten as to likability and familiarity. Those responses are later fed into a computer along with the individual's demographic data, which is converted into an ungodly thick document consisting of numbers, charts, graphs and other information that will eventually be analyzed and overanalyzed. Cost to the radio station? Generally, in the $100,000-plus range. Keep in mind: this is big business. Companies with names like "Hooks Unlimited" exist for the sole purpose of conducting this sort of research for radio stations all over the country. Then, depending on what the final numbers say, songs will get either more or less airplay, or might be dropped from the playlist altogether.

These types of gatherings also give researchers an opportunity to ask a few questions about local radio personalities. Since the group of respondents in the auditorium is under the impression they're taking part in an "independent" study, the provocateur conducting the survey can get away with asking a question like: "What do you think of that J.C. Corcoran?" and get relatively honest responses.

Whatever the results of KLOU's music test were in the summer of 2002, they weren't good. It was as if all support for the station came to a complete halt. We could feel it. There was no question in any of our minds that something was coming down.

Chapter 3

"So I took off my hat and said, 'Imagine that. Me workin' for you.'"
"Signs"
Five Man Electrical Band

Over the course of my nearly three decades in radio I've worked for more than a dozen broadcast companies. Each had its own, individual quirks, upsides and downsides. Some insisted they be viewed as people-oriented, family-style operations, while others reveled in the idea that they were enormous, multi-million-dollar corporate behemoths.

Clear Channel, owners of three St. Louis area "urban" stations along with country-formatted "The Bull," pop and hip-hop entity "Z-107.7" and KLOU, was my least favorite kind of company. I've worked for a lot more employee-friendly outfits in my time. None of us had any illusions about the fact we were mere cogs in a global machine so big and with so many financial, corporate, and even political interests that it was difficult to view one's job there as anything other than temporary.

The company has been a frequent target of journalistic investigations and exposés. In 2002, TV's Public Broadcasting illustrated how Clear Channel's ownership of both concert venues and ticket outlets, coupled with its enormous broadcast empire of 1200 radio stations, produced a virtual monopoly in a growing number of cities. That juggernaut has resulted in a hike of as much as $15 per ticket for shows in some markets. Artists touring the country quickly got the message. Deal with Clear Channel or deal with the consequences.

As if we needed any additional reminder of the arrogance that typified their daily operation, the company president often gave interviews to trade publications in which he made it clear to the industry, not to mention his employees, that if we as on-air talent couldn't figure out a way to perform to the level of spectacular, we might as well get out of the business. A bastion of right-wing political activism, Clear Channel touted worldwide ownership rights to everyone from Dr. Laura Schlesinger to Rush Limbaugh.

"Division" might best describe the company's problem in St. Louis. The three urban stations as well as the entire corporate offices were located in Creve Coeur, but the other three stations, including KLOU, were at 20th and Pine streets, downtown, with our broadcast studios on the second floor but sales and management on the fourth floor. The separation often bred contempt.

I made it a habit of going up to the fourth floor on a daily basis just to keep a tab on what was going on involving the inner workings of the station. Since the management team had to split its time between the two locations, the station manager's executive secretary and office manager, a woman many described as a textbook passive-aggressive control freak and a professional pain-in-the-ass, was left to run the office. Once, upon hearing the Rams' magnetized schedules had arrived, I went up to see about getting a few boxes for us to use in on-air giveaways. She gave me three and shooshed me along. Not three boxes. Three schedules.

Another time she charged into the office I shared with Karen and Brian and began screaming at the top of her lungs about something I'd said on the air that morning about *cats*. When I told her I thought she was way out of line, she just got more emotional, adding crying and a beet-red face to the demonstration. Not knowing what to do or how to stop her, I got up and went down the exterior office hallway to the men's room where I waited for a few minutes, only to find her waiting with more when I came out. Hearing all of the ruckus, a manager finally appeared on the scene and politely suggested we both shut the f*** up!

I could see it coming. It was going to get all over town that "JC started an angry confrontation with a defenseless female co-worker." To my surprise, and probably only because I had witnesses who saw Miss Congeniality go off on me for no reason, she was forced to apologize the next day.

Incidentally, the remark that apparently set her off had something to do with a conversation we'd had on the air about the fascination most kids have with a cat's unique ability to land on its feet, even when suspended upside down from a very low altitude, and how we, as kids, kept reducing that altitude until the cat could no longer flip right side up fast enough. In her view, this was tantamount to endorsing animal cruelty. I wish you could have seen the dumb expression of surprise when I informed her I was a lifelong cat owner and lover.

In early 2001, roughly a year into our stay at KLOU, a manager we felt was one of our strongest allies and confidants got squeezed out of the company. She was replaced by what might as well have been the bastard son of fictional *WKRP in Cincinnati* Director of Sales Herb Tarlek. From day one, it was a classic clash of personality, style, direction, and culture. Since the station's sales had been sluggish, he apparently felt he could do whatever he wanted to correct the situation. Unfortunately, that often compromised our efforts.

The situation was complicated by the fact that a major feud developed between him and our immediate supervisor, the program manager, largely over the issue of Smash. Our boss had long concluded that Smash's effectiveness as an on-air personality had waned, and he wanted him off the air at KLOU. The new sales manager loved Smash, frequently crashed his show in the afternoon, liked the fact that Smash's band could entertain clients in the hospitality tent before Rams games, and wasn't shy about voicing his belief that Smash should be doing the morning show we occupied at KLOU.

Who was going to win this battle for power, we wondered. The guy who controlled the programming or the guy who controlled the money? People were forced to choose sides while the feud went unchecked or possibly even unnoticed by the station manager, who made only occasional appearances in our building.

While all this was happening during the summer of 2001, my lawyer, Jeff Gershman, had been quietly negotiating a new contract extension for me. In August, I took Jeff to his first-ever game at Wrigley Field between the Cardinals and Cubs to celebrate the deal that had been formally agreed to by both sides that would pay me a lot of money over the next three years. While the official papers were being drawn up, I came back after the Labor Day weekend geared up for the beginning of another season of Rams football on KLOU and the all-important fall rating period.

Almost as important, I finally found a terrific house in University City that would finally get me out of the tiny, 900-square-foot condo I'd been crammed into since my divorce in 1999.

But, as one of my heroes, Chicago Bears Hall of Famer Walter Payton once said, "The best week of my life and the worst week of my life were only a week apart."

Chapter 4

"It's alright. It's alright. For we've lived so well so long.
Still when I think of the road we're travelin' on
I wonder what's gone wrong."
"An American Tune"
Paul Simon

Someone at Clear Channel's headquarters outside of Cincinnati got a whiff of the contract we had all agreed to and didn't like it. All along, my lawyer had been under the impression that my boss, the person he was negotiating with, was authorized to speak for the company. It became apparent he was being overruled by somebody at corporate.

This was over-the-top arrogance even by Clear Channel's standards. How could I ever expect even a minimum amount of respect in future dealings if I let them pull an agreed-to contract off the table? In addition, the legal fees that had piled up during the months and months of negotiations amounted to a small fortune. Now, not only was my continued involvement with KLOU in question but there were legal implications, too. A verbal agreement along with a handshake can constitute a legally binding contract in the state of Missouri. As you might expect, as the days went on and nobody at Clear Channel made much of an effort to address the issue, the whole thing began to smolder. I made my best effort to conceal my anger and frustration, but inside, I was doing a slow burn. Karen and Brian knew something was up, and it's always been my policy to be completely honest with my partners about internal issues that might directly affect them.

One morning after the show in early September I closed the door to our office and told them what had happened. I recall that their reactions ranged from concern to irritation. My attorney called a few days later after another conversation with company officials that had not gone well. In the past, I'd seen things like this blow sky high nearly overnight. I came back to the station late that night and retrieved several boxes of files, belongings, and personal effects.

September 11, 2001, began as any other day. We had Cardinals second-baseman Fernando Vina scheduled for his usual Tuesday morning segment along with lots of talk about Tiger Woods' arrival for the big pro golf tournament at Bellerive Country Club in West County, as well as a surprise call to former KMOV meteorologist Trish Brown in Lincoln, Nebraska on her 35th birthday. I'd also planned to talk about a movie screening I'd been to the night before called "Big Trouble," a very funny farce based on a Dave Barry book in which a pair of hapless criminals successfully slip a bomb past an equally hapless guard at the Miami airport security checkpoint.

In the old days, station management sternly outlawed televisions inside radio studios, presumably because they thought we would just sit there and watch *Three's Company* and not pay attention to what we were supposed to be doing. In recent years that thinking changed, and, in fact, we had a good-sized TV hanging from the ceiling to my right in the corner of the KLOU on-air studio.

At about 7:50 a.m. I was in the middle of a phone call with a guy who was talking about the new *Lord of the Rings* movie when Karen and Brian, who stood to my left facing the TV, directed my attention to the first, terrible image from New York.

To this day, listeners still ask how I knew — just moments after the initial pictures of the first plane to collide with the tower were telecast — that this was no accident, and that it was part of a terrorist attack.

The answer? I just knew.

Between 1985 and 1998 I traveled to New York over 150 times and knew the approach to LaGuardia like the back of my hand. The fact that the first plane had made such a precise, direct hit was the primary reason I was so certain of my assessment. Of course I was right, and when the second plane hit, nobody questioned it any further.

We stayed on the air for eight-and-a-half hours on 9-11. Karen and Brian were magnificent that day. In those first few hours I could tell from the ashen look on Karen's face, as she shuttled back and forth from the studio to the news wire down the hall, just how bad things were getting. Each time she would hand me the printed version of the latest development. Each time I would read it on the air. Each time we would search for the appropriate words. Each time we knew there weren't any.

The three of us filled the time with commentary and talked with stunned callers while I simultaneously scanned the hundred or so DirecTV channels that were providing coverage and information. Since we had the TV wired to the control board, I had the ability to put audio on the air at a moment's notice, often describing as best I could what we were seeing on the screen.

Over the course of the following month or two I received close to a thousand e-mail messages from listeners who caught some part of that broadcast, many with their own, personal story of how we got them through the day. (I kept every single one, by the way.) But, regardless of how their stories varied, the single element that repeated itself in nearly all of those messages was that our 9-11 coverage might have been our finest hour. Many people simply thanked us for caring enough to do such a thorough job. Even publications not known for handing out compliments — especially to us — singled us out for special mention.

Life went on for everyone the following day. But I got an additional dose of reality when my attorney called after the show with yet another update on my deteriorating situation with Clear Channel. The saber-rattling had elevated to the point where threats of pulling me off the air until the matter was resolved entered into the discussion.

Without knowing any of this was going on, our marketing and promotions people came in to tell us about an enormous rally and candlelight vigil all six of the St. Louis Clear Channel stations were staging downtown at Kiener Plaza the next night. I anticipated the extravaganza would include politicians, speeches, flag-waving, and patriotic music. Because of the company's strong, conservative roots and ties to the Bush family, I also expected a decidedly pro-Bush, pro-America, pro-let's-go-bomb-the-first-country-with-brown-people-in-it-we-can-find stance, not to mention blasting that obnoxious Lee Greenwood song all over the place. ("God Bless the USA," incidentally, by that time had become, for all intents and purposes, a Republican party anthem, having been performed dozens and dozens of times by Greenwood, himself, at Bush senior *and* junior campaign appearances for several years. More on this later.)

I had three problems. First, I felt nauseated because of what seemed to me like an attempt to make the 9-11 tragedy into a radio station promotion. Second, instead of standing around at Kiener Plaza all night, I felt my time was better spent continuing to monitor the television coverage of what was still a breaking news event. Third, my ties to this company were looking very, very frayed.

It was now Friday morning, and I felt a distinct chill in the room. When we got off the air, Brian closed the door to our office, and he and Karen ripped into me for not having attended the event the night before. I tried to explain that if *my* situation wasn't good, *their* situation wasn't good, but that reasoning seemed to fall upon deaf ears. The conversation continued to deteriorate when what appeared to be a long list of issues unrelated to the events of that week began to surface.

I got a call from the station program director on Sunday morning. Apparently a series of talks had taken place and phone calls exchanged throughout the first part of the weekend and a meeting was being called for three o'clock involving the four of us. Fans will never know how close the show came to ending that afternoon.

Largely because of the even-tempered handling of the situation by our program director, all three of us who'd had our professional and personal friendship tested to the max came out of the meeting alive and with that friendship — as well as our show — still intact.

A few days later the station manager we rarely saw in our building ran into me in the downstairs lobby. He reassured me that he was aware of everything that had been going on and then put his arm around me and told me everything was "going to work out just fine."

At a staff meeting of all six stations Thursday, September 28th at Maggie O'Brien's, a sales manager from one of our sister stations surprised all of us when he stood up in front of the hundred-plus employees and singled out our show for our 9-11 coverage. Then, in a clumsy, awkward moment the station manager interjected, "Well, I think *all* of our stations did an admirable job."

Hmmmm.

The following Sunday, less than three weeks after the 9-11 attacks, I flew into New York's LaGuardia airport in what could only be described as a near out-of-body experience. Most people in this country wouldn't have dreamed of even getting near an airport, let alone flying into Ground Zero territory. I was there to broadcast from a live, nationally televised tribute concert to John Lennon that had been postponed from an earlier date due to the attacks. I picked up my pal, Chris Albers, a St. Louis native and writer for *Late Night with Conan O'Brien*, and headed over to the theater.

When I got back, there was a message waiting for me from Jeff, my attorney. Clear Channel was now offering a greatly reduced, one-year deal.

And just as that development occurred, the house deal fell through. That meant I'd be stuck in the condo for another year, and it threw my attempts to stabilize a relationship I was in at the time into disarray and worked against the best interests of my two young daughters.

Jeff's calls to station management largely went unreturned for the balance of 2001. Without the security that comes with a contract, I continued to do my job, honoring my commitments, and I fully participated in all station activities. I volunteered for a series of nonpaying appearances for the station. I helped organize and host the "Cans Film Festival" with the Salvation Army and Wehrenberg Theaters at Christmas. I saw less and less of upper management and less and less of my boss who, I surmised, was mortified by what he was watching his company do to me.

While I was in New Orleans at the Rams' Super Bowl appearance in February of 2002, I received a message that my spring training broadcasts from Florida scheduled for the following month were being canceled.

On Friday, February 15, the program director asked to see me in his office after the show. When I walked in I was quite surprised to see the station manager and the company's human resources director in the room. Behind a closed door, the station manager began a prepared, termination speech taking me to task for "refusing to adhere to station policy even after repeated written warnings." About 30 seconds into it, I simply said, "STOP!"

"What policy? What written warnings?" I asked.

I was told my e-mail responses to a listener who had been sending me increasingly creepy and threatening messages was at the heart of the matter, and that my refusal to follow the policy repeatedly e-mailed to me by the company was cause for termination.

There was just one problem. Since we had only one computer in a small office shared by three people, I never even used the company system and, in fact, operated my own Web site and e-mail system from my home. I told them I didn't even know what my Clear Channel e-mail address *was* and invited them to bring it up on-screen so they could see no messages had ever even been so much as accessed.

The three managers in the room were clearly stunned. I was told I was free to go, but I knew what had just happened was a failed attempt on the part of Clear Channel to manufacture a case against me that would legally allow them to dismiss me for "cause."

I had worked very hard; I'd done everything asked of me; I'd gotten decent results, particularly given the situation; and I'd not given them any real trouble. If they wanted to get rid of me, fine, though it's sort of pathetic to think that this mega-company that liked to view itself as progressive, cutting-edge, and visionary couldn't figure out how to build around an 18-year veteran of the market with a built-in audience. Were their lawyers fearful I'd sue over the "disappearing contract trick" they had pulled a few months earlier and, thus, attempting to cover their tracks? All I really knew is what they were trying to pull was just plain *dirty*.

The following Friday, again, the program director asked to see me in his office after the show and, again, the same group was waiting for me.

"We're going in a new direction with the station, and you're not part of it," I was told by the station manager. I was instructed to sign a small stack of termination papers but referred them to my lawyer. Karen and Brian helped me clean out my office over the weekend. A few days later when all the paperwork arrived at my attorney's office, it was all dated "February 15, 2002." They hadn't even gone to the trouble to change it from the original, bogus date on which they had tried to terminate me for "cause" a week earlier. My two-year stint at KLOU was over.

Chapter 5

"Hello, it's me. I'm not at home. If you'd like to reach me, leave me alone."
"Change"
Sheryl Crow

The following week, Smash reappeared in morning drive with Karen Kelly and Brian McKenna along with a new format, something called "Superhits of the '60s and '70s," which consisted of lots of ballads from Barry Manilow, country crossovers from Eddie Rabbit, and an ungodly amount of disco. Later I learned the format was described as a "companywide experiment" that had been launched on, and in some cases forced upon, close to a dozen Clear Channel stations across the country.

As the previous year's winner of the St. Louis Air Awards "Lifetime Achievement Award," I had already accepted the task of delivering the introductory speech for Mark Klose's induction two weeks later at the Pageant. My reception by the crowd — made up almost entirely of people from the local radio industry — was, to say the least, "cool." I made matters worse by taking a few swipes at my former employer onstage and by delivering my speech in a "roast" style.

> "Mark Klose's first job at KSHE 30 years ago was to pass out bumper stickers. He must have done a pretty good job, too, because a lot of them are still on those cars his listeners drive! Those things are harder to get off than Anne Keefe after a pitcher of martinis!"

The material was met with almost dead silence. They didn't get what I was doing. Maybe they didn't want to get it. All I knew was that my name was mud. I drove home and wondered about what to do next.

Things remained very quiet until the final week of March when my e-mail lit up like a Christmas tree, and my phone began ringing like crazy. Everybody had the same question. Was I about to return to KLOU on

Monday morning?

It took me about 30 seconds to figure out that Smash was pulling a variation of the same stunt he'd perpetrated almost 10 years prior while at KSHE. The Monday in question was the first day of the season for the Cardinals, the day I traditionally present my massive, opening day baseball special. Smash, Karen, and Brian were proclaiming on the air that "a very familiar voice is about to return to the morning show on Monday." They continued, "He's had some trouble in the past, but he's worked things out with management and...well...you know what Monday is, right?" Listeners heard that, looked at the schedule, put two and two together and naturally assumed it meant I was about to make a triumphant return. Of course, that's just what KLOU wanted them to believe.

On Monday, April 1, 2002 — "April Fools Day" — listeners heard Smash re-introduce... "Mr. Tic-Toc," an electronically generated voice produced by pushing a button on a novelty clock Smash had used on the air regularly at KSHE a dozen years prior.

The idea backfired. People weren't just pissed. They were furious. I even had to calm down some listeners who thought *I'd* had something to do with the whole thing. It had been a long time since I'd seen my audience *that* angry.

Over the next few months, tension would mount in the KLOU studios. Karen and Brian, who had been close friends in and out of the station, stopped seeing eye-to-eye regarding the direction of the show. Soon after, Brian was let go as management made one last stab at salvaging something — anything — from what remained of the original lineup. Karen and Smash limped along for several more months. Then, over the Christmas, 2002 break, KLOU pulled the plug on Karen, Smash, and the entire morning show, opting instead to return to a traditional oldies format with music from 6 to 10 each morning.

It's not uncommon these days for a person to lose his job, even if he's performing to expectation. We've all seen and read heart-wrenching stories about the stereotypical "little guy" who loses his job, maybe even his home and family, when the tragedy of unemployment strikes. And that's what it is, too. A tragedy. The studies and research show that a person losing his livelihood often produces unparalleled devastation.

When a public person loses his job, I believe that devastation multiplies exponentially if for no other reason than it happens in full view of everyone. For some reason, all of the long faces and compassion exhibited during the story about that "little guy" seem to disappear. Somehow, that empathy for the loss of livelihood seems undeserved. Enemies rejoice. Neighbors mumble. Competitors snicker. But, it's no less tragic. In fact it's worse. Swarms of gossipmongers, chat-room cheetahs and professional know-nothings begin cackling with claims of "insider information," "sources deep inside the station" and an insidious insistence that only *they* possess the behind-the-scenes knowledge necessary to tell you what *really* happened. They're almost always clueless as to the complexity of the situation. We laugh at former Blues great Brian Sutter when he said: "It's part of the game. Trades are part of the game. People get fired; it's part of the game. Peoples' contracts not getting renewed is part of the game. It's an unfortunate part of the game, but it is part of the game." In a clumsy, convoluted way, he had it right. Chances are, there was a helluva lot more going on than anyone not directly involved in the situation could ever know.

What becomes of one's career in this business is often the result of a bizarre equation involving corporate capriciousness, format changes, salary dumping, signal strength, politics, advertising, marketing, trends, consultants, more politics...and occasionally talent.

Chapter 6

"And I feel like I've been here before."
"Déjà Vu"
Crosby, Stills, Nash & Young

I'm not very good at keeping secrets, and in the summer of 2002, I had to keep one for a very, very long time.

The first thing I did after getting dumped by KLOU was to get on the phone with anyone who would talk to me to try and launch a preemptive strike. I had to confront all of the goons who never fail to use opportunities like this to flood the discussion with manufactured stories suggesting my departure might have been due to misconduct or any other lie they think they might be able to get away with. I also started asking lots of questions about what possibilities might exist for something to open up. Of course, the massive deregulation of the broadcast industry that took place in the late nineties now meant that the dozen or so companies that had owned radio stations in St. Louis now was reduced to just a handful. I'd just parted with a company that operates six stations in town, so I had to count all of them out, and almost all of the remaining big stations either already had a morning show firmly in place or presented some other obstacle pertaining to my potential employment.

I got as far as lunch with the guy who was now in charge of programming for KMOX. He had been a manager at KTRS and was instrumental in getting me hired there in 1999. Though he was now trying to decide what to do about sinking ratings on two of his daytime shows, two things stood in the way of our doing a deal. First, the guy they were thinking about replacing still had almost a year left on his contract. Second, the woman who was now vice president and general manager of the station was no longer willing to give me the time of day following a falling-out we'd had at KSD in 1998. Still, I was told my name would be on the short list when it was time to make a change. This information, while appreciated, did me no good.

It was at that lunch that I asked KMOX's programming chief about a promo line I'd been hearing on the show KMOV's Larry Conners was doing each afternoon between 2 and 3 p.m.: *"And now, back to St. Louis' most-respected journalist...Larry Conners."*

Surveys, research studies, and even polls are being conducted in St. Louis all the time, but I hadn't heard of anything along these lines. So I asked what market study they were quoting that showed Conners had achieved such elite status. "Larry wrote it," he said.

Duh.

Another local station general manager offered to help me find a job in any way she could...as long as it was out of town.

Thanks.

I received a very encouraging phone call from Bob Costas within a day or two. For a guy with a day-planner full of international commitments to have taken time out to try and boost my spirits is something rare, though I've always suspected Eric Mink, a pal of both Bob and me, called him and asked if he'd help try and talk me in off the ledge.

You may recall in *Real Life Stories of J.C. and The Breakfast Club or Twenty Minutes in the Dark with Madonna* I detailed the hostile, creepy treatment I was always on the receiving end of from former *Riverfront Times* columnist, Richard Byrne. Over a 10-year period he misrepresented, mischaracterized, and attacked virtually every move I made, while carefully omitting any story that might have portrayed me in a positive light. But Byrne, who'd had a public falling-out with his former collaborator and my other favorite *RFT* jackass, Thomas Crone, had now been rid of St. Louis for several years, having fled to the nation's capital for another newspaper job. That's probably why I was so surprised when I began reading an e-mail with his name on it that had popped up on my computer screen. In the note he ridiculed me for having been cut from the KLOU lineup and hurled some other insults in my direction that reminded me of the "nah nah nah nah nah nah" days on my grade school playground. When I activated an e-mail blocker which effectively stopped any more of his messages from reaching me, Byrne quickly sent me two more by using a pair of alternate Internet accounts.

There are creeps, and then there are *creeps.*

A few days after I'd left KLOU my pal Trish Gazall at The River invited me to come onto her morning show to "say goodbye" to my audience, tell my side of the story and, of course, to get a ton of publicity for her station. In fact, Trish and I had numerous conversations over the years in which she expressed strong interest in doing a show together. I also knew that she'd had the same kind of conversation with her bosses, including one guy who'd been our sales manager in the old KSD days, as well as their new program director from Chicago, with whom I struck up an immediate friendship. So, when I took to the airwaves that morning on 101.1, I viewed it as a kind of "audition."

The show went very well.

Not a thing came of it.

At that point the writing was on the wall, and I knew what I had to do.

Now, I documented in great detail my unceremonious parting with KSHE and Emmis Broadcasting in 1986 in *Real Life Stories of JC and The Breakfast Club or Twenty Minutes in the Dark with Madonna.* As regrettable at that was, what followed after I became their direct competitor at KSD from 1987 to 1991 was much, much worse. Listeners will recall how both sides sunk to a near-daily diatribe of name-calling, personal insults, and terrible accusations that seemed to become more personal as time went on. What made things worse was the fact that it resulted not only in the breakup of one of the most-successful morning teams in St. Louis radio history but also my friendship with John Ulett.

But in recent years John and I had been spending lots of time together, usually in the public address announcer booth he shares with Busch Stadium organist Ernie Hays. We would also see each other at industry functions around town and on the road at spring training as well as post-season play for both the Cardinals and the Rams. It was during these very, very long talks that I discovered just how much admiration John had for my work as a broadcaster. I guess I just never really knew.

John insisted (and, by the way, still insists) I should be hosting a politically oriented show and often said that I could become a nationally syndicated, ideological alternative to Rush Limbaugh. I always responded kindly but also indicated that I don't even like politics — that I felt a fondness for politics would be absolutely necessary to be effective in that kind of role.

I spent a lot of time with U-Man when my stint at KLOU was nearing its end at the Rams' 2002 appearance in the Super Bowl in New Orleans. On the Friday night before the game we got away from the crowd and enjoyed a traditional Cajun meal in a restaurant near the French Quarter. I guess I should say *I* "enjoyed" it. John, as usual, seemed to inspect and scrutinize every spoonful with a great deal of suspicion.

I told John about how miserable an operation KLOU had become, that I was having serious contract trouble, and that I wasn't sure what was going to happen when my deal was up in a few months. But I distinctly remember two things about that evening. I picked up the first indication that Emmis Broadcasting (operators of KSHE, K-HITS, The Mall, The Point, and 97.1) might be reassessing its view of the "Steve & DC" morning show. I sensed John sort of taking my temperature about personal matters, my current state of mind, and where my head was at these days. Did John know something? Was John trying to decide if he should go to his bosses and push the idea of my returning to Emmis?

Security at the New Orleans Superdome was extraordinary in the wake of the September 11 attacks just five-and-a-half months earlier. In spite of the fact that I was covering the game for KLOU, the flagship station of the Rams Radio Network, John, who had applied for media credentials at the last minute, ended up with much better seats than I had in the converted press area. As fate would have it, there was a no-show next to him so he waved me over. To our right was a young, attractive woman in her early twenties adorned from head to toe in New England Patriots garb. Since this is considered a real "no no" in a press area, we ridiculed her throughout the game and, in the process, learned she worked for a satellite news service based in Boston aimed at grade-school kids. John and I had a lot of laughs at her expense that day until, of course, we had to helplessly stand by as Mike Martz proceeded to give away the game. (By the way, about six months later that young woman sitting next to us would be announced as the new, superstar reporter for *Entertainment Tonight*, Maria Menounos.)

John and I shook hands after the Rams' 20-17 loss and vowed to stay in touch.

When KLOU pulled the plug on my show just a few weeks later on February 22, 2002, U-Man was the first person I called. Over the course of the next few weeks, John would encourage me to attempt to repair my relationship with Emmis Broadcasting. Odd as it may seem in the current climate of the broadcast industry, the three principle players that headed up the company at the time of my split in 1986 were still running the operation: General Manager John Beck, Operations Manager Rick Balis, and President Rick Cummings (who had recently been elevated to that position). If that final name sounds familiar, allow me to cannibalize from my first book as a way of refreshing your memory:

> "The...meeting took place in General Manager John Beck's office in the prefab sales and management adjacent to the KSHE studios. The agenda was made abundantly clear. The programming geniuses in Indianapolis had decided KSHE should move to a more mainstream sound, and new songs by Prince and Madonna were about to be added to the playlist. And they were counting on me to sell it to the KSHE audience.
>
> For the next ninety minutes, all you could hear was the sound of four grown men screaming at one another.
>
> The company president and his programming 'expert' insisted these songs would broaden the station's appeal. I, in turn, suggested the two admit themselves to a state hospital. After more than an hour of this, I offered to make a deal. I told them I'd do what they wanted if they gave me a company car. Completely baffled, they asked why. I answered, 'If I play Prince and Madonna records on KSHE, listeners are going to turn my car over in the parking lot. I want it to be yours, not mine.'
>
> They were not amused."

So, here it is 16 years later and Rick Cummings, the guy I'd semi-sarcastically referred to in the book as an "expert" and "programming genius" was now president of the company...and Ulett thought I ought to just give him a ring.

The message I left at his office in southern California went unanswered. I recall not being surprised. I also recall wondering if this was finally it for me in St. Louis.

A few days later the phone rang. A surprisingly upbeat Rick Cummings and I talked for well over an hour, covering everything from radio to kids and all points in between. That was the good news. The bad news was that Rick didn't feel it was his place to meddle in such a sensitive area with the relatively autonomously run Emmis St. Louis properties. Translated? My problem was going to be Operations Manager Rick Balis.

By the time I'd left KSHE in November of 1986, I couldn't tell if Rick just hated me or was simply exhausted by the continual stream of "issues" that had become a by-product of my show. Toss in the *real* bad blood that was generated *after* I'd jumped to competitor KSD, and it wouldn't have puzzled most people as to why the door seemed to be nailed shut. Interestingly, I'd had a chance encounter with Rick on a short MetroLink ride back from the ballpark one afternoon in 1999 and used the opportunity to make a clumsy attempt at an apology. Rick was polite, but I was left with a sort of "no dice" feeling.

I got a cool reception from Rick Balis when I reached him a few weeks later. Something told me, though, that if I could keep him on the phone long enough I might just have a shot. As was the case during my call to the company president, the conversation wove its way through topics unrelated to the business like kids, divorce (which we'd both just gone through), and what the last 16 years had been like for each of us. I felt the tone of the conversation shift ever so slightly in the final minutes of what was now a nearly two-hour call.

Weeks went by.

I was with my daughters at their annual school carnival Memorial Day weekend of 2002 when my phone rang. It was John Beck.

In a fashion that might best be described as cryptic he glossed over a scenario that would have me returning to one of the Emmis stations, though he said I would have to be patient and that he wasn't at liberty to tell me when, which station he had in mind, or any other details.

A few weeks later I was asked to meet with the two managers of Emmis' talk station and K-HITS 96. I didn't get much of an idea what was up their collective sleeves at that lunch, though we talked about several different potential openings at the talk station and very little about K-HITS. But I was hearing rumblings about the company's growing concern over the continuing ratings nosedive for Steve & DC's show. Without any significant, competitive changes in the morning drive landscape in St. Louis, the duo had fallen from first place to as low as tenth.

It was another month before John Beck finally spilled the beans. An extremely complicated and confidential plan was in place that would have me take over the K-HITS morning show sometime in early fall of 2002. John knew things were going to get sticky with Steve & DC and that any part of the plan could conceivably blow sky high. I was on pins and needles because I'd seen many sure-thing deals that were only hours away from completion go up in smoke.

So, for a good portion of the summer of 2002 I had to sit quietly and ponder the staggering irony of my replacing a fallen Steve & DC. These were the two guys who had made verbal attacks on my baby daughter a staple of their show for years, planned and executed a physical attack on me in 1994 that resulted in a lawsuit in which I was awarded $370,000 by a St. Louis jury, and who had generally been responsible for some of the most questionable personal and career choices in local radio history.

I also had to start thinking about what I was going to do about getting co-hosts, a producer, sports person, etc. — a task made more difficult by the fact that the whole thing was such a secret and because I had no idea what resources I'd have to work with. On top of that, we hadn't even worked out a contract with the station. I began to wonder how I was supposed to pull all of these loose ends together and get a top-notch show on the air in just a few months.

On August 7 I met John Beck and Rick Balis for lunch at a Kirkwood eatery. It was then that John dropped the bomb of the century: their plan was to move Steve & DC to the weaker-signaled, adult-contemporary station known as The Mall. I would take over the K-HITS morning show...with John Ulett. Whatever they said for the next few minutes I'll never know because I was just *floored*. There hadn't been so much as the slightest indication that this was their plan. I called my girlfriend, my family, and a few close friends I knew I could trust. They all knew this was going to be more than just another show on another radio station. This had a chance to be very big.

Over the next few weeks U-Man and I would talk many times about the new show. After all, we hadn't been on the air together in sixteen years, and there was a lot to cover.

The original plan was for Fox2's Margie Ellisor, who was already splitting her time reading news for Steve & DC's show as well as K-HITS, to move over to our show full-time. But we got our first setback when she told management she wanted to stay with Steve & DC, presumably so that her family in Minnesota could continue to hear her on a tiny station that was part of their syndication network. We approached an eager Deanne Lane, but KSDK management nixed the deal out of concern her involvement "might harm her hard news image." Now it was only a few days before our debut and the decision was made to have John perform double-duty as co-host and newsman.

Once Margie was no longer in the picture, Jennifer Sparks, who also was part of the Emmis stable of talent, became more interested in becoming part of the show. Fox2 meteorologist Dave Murray had been part of the previous show, and I think I surprised station management by asking that we keep him on. But I'd seen enough research indicating he was perceived as the top weather guy in town — I knew his presence would add some credibility to the show — and we'd worked together briefly at KMOX. Oh, yeah. And I am *TWISTER BOY!!!*

Without an office, a desk, a computer, a phone, or a producer, we launched the new show on Monday, September 16, 2002. Management speculated it might take a few weeks — or even a few months — for us to regain our timing and chemistry. But at 6 a.m. when it became apparent John's microphone hadn't been properly connected, we were immediately plunged into official broadcast chaos and had to improvise our way out of it.

It was as if we'd only been apart for a weekend. It even surprised us that our act and our timing had remained intact.

Laurie Mac gave her notice at Clear Channel about a week later and joined us two weeks after that. That was a good thing, too, because things hit full speed almost immediately. Paul McCartney was scheduled to play the Savvis Center in a few weeks, so after being on the air on K-HITS for only a week, I found myself in Minneapolis previewing the concert and doing the radio show from there the following morning. And only a week later the Cardinals were in the playoffs, so John and I were on our way to cover the games from Arizona and subsequently San Francisco. In retrospect, we'd caught an enormous break having all of these marquee events going on at a time when we were trying to draw attention to the new show. Throw in a very clever $300,0000 TV campaign showing famous album covers with John's and my head superimposed over the musicians' faces, and we could almost feel the audience growing.

I've learned a lot of things the hard way in the last 20 years, and one of them is that you can't do it alone. Any show, regardless of how effective it is, still only constitutes a mere *one-sixth* of the broadcast day. So, unless you have talented and dedicated people who are given the opportunity by management to display that talent and dedication, you have very little. But in the case of K-HITS it was beginning to look as though we had it all, with Mark Klose in the afternoon, market veteran Drew Johnson at night, and the amazing Radio Rich Dalton following us at ten o'clock. Add some decent weekenders, a pair of feisty marketing and promotion people and, of course, the incomparable Carl the Intern working behind-the-scenes, and it simply didn't occur to us that the operation wouldn't succeed.

The ratings began to move in the late fall of 2002, but the increase didn't seem to be coming fast enough for any of us. Then, at daybreak the first week of December, a peculiar mix of snow, freezing rain, and sleet descended upon the area. We capitalized on the situation with four full hours of coverage that ranged from critical information about traffic tie-ups and dozens of school and holiday event cancellations to hilarious cell phone calls from commuters stuck for hours on area roads. The phones went wild with what seemed like each caller trying to outdo the one before with "creative" observations about St. Louis' bizarre overreaction to foul winter weather. One listener described in detail his odyssey of being stuck on I-70 so long that he resorted to getting out of his car and walking across a service road to a convenience store only to return 20 minutes later to traffic that hadn't moved an inch. Another caller checked in with regular updates about how he felt he was being "mocked" by the rhythmic movement of the wiper blades of the motorist alongside him.

On that December day, we kicked the crap out of Bob & Tom, Howard Stern, and the other syndicated morning shows that simply were in no position to deal with this local situation as we did. The show had left our abdominal muscles aching from laughter. Afterwards, I shared with Laurie Mac and Program Director Rick Balis my belief that this had been a pivotal day in both the show's history and the station's history.

February 2003 produced a hilarious contest in which listeners were asked to compose a song, poem, comedy routine, or presentation for a chance to win one of five trips to the Bahamas. The winners were entertaining. Some of the non-winners were much more so. That was followed by a great spring training trip, opening day, our annual pilgrimage to Chicago for the Cubs-Cards weekend at Wrigley Field, a very busy June that included several days of live broadcasts from Disney World, Yankee Stadium, and Fenway Park in Boston. Before we knew it, we were doing Rams tailgate parties. The ratings were exploding off the page.

For many years, *St. Louis Magazine* had held its annual "singles night" at the Ritz-Carlton in Clayton on the night before Thanksgiving. The crowd usually hovered around 400 to 600 people. But in the fall of 2003, the popular publication decided to work with us for the first time. We ran a short series of very creative and funny contests, gave away lots of tickets, and generally made it sound like the social event of the year. As I approached the place near the intersection of Hanley and Forsyth, there were headlights as far as I could see. The crowd that night was estimated at 1300! I knew the magazine's new, fresh approach had a lot to do with it. But I knew we had a lot to do with it, too.

It was a terrific Christmas special that aired in December with more than a dozen of St. Louis' celebrities and dignitaries taking part. Everyone wanted to be part of the show. It was looking as though we had a real shot at finishing the year in the number one spot. When the ratings were released in mid-January, inexplicably over 30 percent of our audience had simply vanished. Or had it? That's what the numbers said, but we never believed it. The next big ratings book wasn't due for another three months, so we had no choice but to plow ahead and hope the nosedive was a fluke. Besides, I had to begin the gargantuan task of organizing the upcoming 20th anniversary celebration. That meant scrounging through boxes and boxes of tapes of old shows, then listening, editing, and attending meeting after meeting with our promotion, marketing, Internet, and programming people from the station who were absolutely essential to making those two weeks just hum. I saw nothing but the four walls of my office for weeks on end.

On Tuesday, April 27 at noon, just a few days before the 20th anniversary celebration was to begin, I stood over the sales manager's computer printer and watched as a piece of paper slid out showing *The Showgram* with JC, U-Man, Sparky, and Mac had officially hit number one. My top-rated show had been stolen from me in 1991 and I'd been through hell and back trying to re-claim that spot. The debacle of KMOX. The heads-up-their-asses managers and crappy signal of The Fox and

The River. Getting caught in the laughable, revolving door of KTRS. The humiliation and embarrassment of being sold three times in three years by a company that didn't even want us the second go-around at KSD. And what could those guys at Clear Channel be thinking now? I would later tell Deb Peterson at the *Post-Dispatch*: "This is a 13-year-long monkey off my back."

Chapter 7

"I can't complain but sometimes I still do."
"Life's Been Good"
Joe Walsh

Whether or not I think we've just done a good show usually has a lot to do with my mood for the rest of the day. The good news is that these days the killer-to-stinker ratio is the best it's ever been. In fact, it's not unusual for me to go as long as two weeks before I have to admit a show we've just completed wasn't good enough to be on the air in Paducah.

The configuration of John, Jen, Mac, and me appears to be the best we've ever had. It's one thing for us to feel that way. It's another thing for our listeners to tell us. And it's something *completely* different hearing it from our management team. Not everyone is cut out for this kind of show. Everything we do is improvisational. In fact, during the show, much of the off-air chatter that goes on in the studio while the commercials are running gets cut off. "Tell me when we go back on," we've each been known to say. It's the only way you can get that first, true reaction. It's one of the main reasons the show sounds different and one of the main reasons our show *is* different from almost anything else of its kind.

The conversation that ensues off-air during the songs and commercials, oftentimes, is indescribable. At any given moment, there might be a highly personal discussion involving family affairs, the latest scuttle about a fellow employee, or serious issues facing the company. Those breaks also give the girls an opportunity to make a cogent observation out of thin air. Something along the lines of: "JC and John are the only two guys we know whose looks actually *improved* with hair loss." But at least once per show that off-air discussion turns to something hilariously vile, filthy, graphic, and disgusting. It's a miracle we're all still able to face one another the next day. On occasion, Sparks, a Catholic girl from a genuinely sweet, south St. Louis family, can have a mouth like a sailor.

The combination of Laurie's smile, command of the English language and southern accent can, when necessary, produce a lethal capacity. U-Man has a tendency to express complete surprise that something he said produced an audible gasp and jaw-dropping response from the girls.

Each of us has a specific set of responsibilities. Each of us has a specific role.

Though Jennifer Sparks' official title is "traffic reporter," her role has many layers. At 27, it's part of her job to make sure John and I never end up sounding like the two old geezers who sat in the balcony on *The Muppet Show*. From almost day one, she and I developed the sort of Maddie Hayes-David Addison-type relationship America grew to love on the '80s television series, *Moonlighting*. I hurl dozens of completely inappropriate comments in her direction, and she systematically shoots them down with deadly precision. Sparks is also the most politically conservative of our group.

U-Man and I talk frequently about how poorly we would do if the situation were reversed. There is *no way* either John or I, at 27, would have been able to hold our own had we been thrust into an environment with a group of more mature and experienced broadcast veterans.

When I met Laurie Mac, her talents were being completely wasted. Though well-known on the local theater circuit as an accomplished actress, she'd recently come off a very disappointing — and some would say aggravating and frustrating — stint co-hosting another local morning show. There her contributions, suggestions, and ideas weren't welcome, and lack of respect was a daily issue, plus support from management was nonexistent.

Laurie had unceremoniously left that show and was assigned at Emmis to pre-record news updates for three different stations each half-hour, all morning long. This meant she sat in a studio by herself and read copy into a computerized system that would automatically fire off the newscasts at the designated time and on the designated show. In other words, there were no creative opportunities, and there was no interaction with any on-air talent. The job seemed just short of a clerical position, and maybe that's why she jumped at the opportunity to join me at K-HITS.

Now Laurie's mornings are more suited to her vast talents and organizational aptitude. It's not uncommon for her to be prepping an upcoming guest, getting names and addresses of contest winners on the phone, reminding me of the details of an upcoming segment, *and* coming up with something brilliant to say on the air...ALL within 30 seconds of one another. A hypoglycemic air traffic controller on Halloween has an easier time of things. On any given day, Mac is the smartest one in the room. This company has no idea what they have in her.

And then there's John "the U-Man" Ulett. I gave him that nickname several weeks after we'd begun working together in 1984 and often referred to him that way on the air. One afternoon back then, Cardinals second baseman Tom Herr saw him outside the clubhouse at Busch Stadium and called out, "Hey U-Man." The name has stuck with him ever since.

I've never had as much difficulty trying to explain what a partner's contribution to the show is as I do with John. If you asked whether he's the funniest, smartest, wackiest, most serious, most self-deprecating, or most complicated, the answer would have to be "yes" and "no."

As a husband and father of three young daughters, John is at a point in his life at which he thinks what he thinks and believes what he believes. Just beneath a thin exterior persona that ranges from friendly, playful, silly, happy-go-lucky, and outgoing to devilish and fun-loving is a complicated, nervous, occasionally uneasy fellow. U-Man's religion is golf. If he's not playing golf he's thinking about playing golf. It still bugs the crap out him that my second-*ever* golf outing (and keep in mind I didn't even have clubs, shoes or any idea how to play) took place at Pebble Beach, arguably one of the most beautiful, expensive, revered courses in the country.

John also tends to be a bit of a hypochondriac. I've often said I could hire an actress to come on the show and pretend to be a nurse who's identifying a new, mystery illness that's sweeping through the region. Within an hour of her departure John would claim to have it.

Though his love of performing and the desire to amass huge sums of money certainly factor into the equation, I think it's John's general lack of calm that accounts for his brutal work ethic. Ask yourself what would motivate someone to keep his outrageously demanding schedule. The minute we separate at 9 each morning, John zips directly down the hall where he hosts the 9 to 1 o'clock show on KSHE. He also does a four-hour show there on Sunday mornings and has a completely separate schedule of remote broadcasts, meetings, and obligations with that station. He gets to go home after seven straight hours on the air, but he does that 25-mile drive from the opposite direction just a few hours later 81 days a year as he returns to Busch Stadium, where he's been the Cardinals' public address announcer for 20 seasons. That means on days the Redbirds are home, John racks up a hundred miles a day in travel. And somewhere in all of that he tries to play golf (his true passion) several times a week while managing to be a dedicated husband and father.

Now, you'll recall that, for the better part of 15 years, I got up at 4 a.m., did a radio show, left for television in the afternoon most days, and traveled to Los Angeles or New York to record movie-related celebrity interviews as many as 30 weekends a year. Still, somehow, I get exhausted even thinking about U-man's schedule.

John gets pretty close to obsessive-compulsive disorder territory, too. On a recent trip to Florida, U-man convinced our group to eat at the same restaurant four of the five nights we were there. It's on these trips that we're likely to become engaged in long, surprisingly candid, deep conversations about kids, politics, and the world in general. Could we possibly be on the air together 40 years from now trying to sell the idea that "ninety is the new seventy?" It's during these talks that it occurs to me how much I missed him during our 16-year separation. How much better a person might I be today had John been around for me to kibbitz with?

Here's one of our typical trips together: U-Man and I were sitting side by side on the flight back from spring training and making fun of the standard preflight announcements. These must be for everyone who hasn't been on a plane since 1965, and they go along great with the seatbelt demonstration for everyone who hasn't been in a car since 1959! The cabin sounds like the maternity ward at Missouri Baptist Hospital. Was there some sort of freakish, post 9-11 baby boom we're both unaware of? We surmise every third seat is occupied by a baby and that there might even be a few more stowed in the overhead compartments. John and I are cracking one joke after another while the stranger in the seat next to me, a very square fellow in his forties wearing a denim shirt with Tweety Pie embroidered on the pocket, is trying unsuccessfully to hold back his laughter. Our giddiness actually began about an hour earlier when I reopened an issue that had surfaced on a trip the year before when John complained that an airport restaurant put *too much* cheese on his pizza.

Who complains about *too much* cheese?

Hardly a moment later John has his nose buried in the financial pages of *USA Today*. (That nose, incidentally, is typically covered by a Breathe-Right nasal strip he frequently wears throughout the day, even during our television appearances. We've been arguing for months about what the correct placement on the nose is. I fear we're going to end up like Johnny Carson and Ed McMahon, who had a 30-year-long feud about which was smarter, a horse or a pig.) Long known by his friends for his money smarts and for the fact that he does all his own investing, he has me convinced he did things the right way and that I did things the wrong way. Instead of my highly publicized fat salaries, on and off again employment, and exorbitant legal expenses, he's handled his affairs in a polar opposite fashion and has all the money to prove it. I've been known to tease him about his impressive home, which I refer to as a "compound," and for the fact that it has a lovely gift shop.

Everyone should be so lucky as to have a pal like John Ulett.

We're hearing that word again. "Chemistry." They say you either have it or you don't. They say John and I have it. Now they're saying the four of us have it together. And, after all these years, I believe I've finally come up with a way to describe my own role on the show. I liken it to a restaurant kitchen.

Every morning when I walk into the building I have a "kitchen" full of ingredients at my fingertips. There are newspapers, magazines, faxes, press releases, letters, e-mail, sound bites, phone messages, and miscellaneous "jock prep" services consisting of show biz news and bizarre news blurbs from around he world. Truthfully, on an average day, as in the restaurant business, 80 percent of what I have access to is the same stuff everyone else has. And, just like in the restaurant business, the quality and style of your meal will still vary greatly...depending upon who the chef is.

That's me.

My job is to begin selecting those individual ingredients, throw them in the pot, crank up the heat and begin stirring tenaciously. If I've done my job right that day, the place may end up with a huge mess, but what I've put on the table for you will be memorable and should make you want to come back for more.

In a lot of ways my day doesn't even begin until I get home and start plowing through the many news, sports, and entertainment programs recorded on one of my three TiVos (which have essentially replaced my much-publicized *nine* VCRs), the Internet, and the over two hundred e-mails I receive virtually every day. But really, I get paid for my instinct. I have to know what to say, when to say it, and how far to go. I have to know the difference between what listeners are going to be interested in hearing us talk about and what's going to make them bored and punch the button for another radio station. Hitting the right sound effect, music theme, or sound bite at the right time can reach the level of high art if done correctly. And then there are the phones. *The Showgram* is unique in that we're the only morning radio program that does not screen calls. It's like a highwire walker working without a net. Barring profanity and slander, anyone can say anything, no matter how complicated the aftermath, and we have to be good enough to handle it. I often think about how few people there are in this business who possess the skill to do this, especially this way. At K-HITS we have five local, incoming lines along with the toll-free line, a "warmline" (used primarily by guests on the show, regular contributors and staff) and a "hotline" used by management in the case of an emergency or when someone feels like yelling at us. When I look down and see all six of those listener lines flashing, I have a pretty good idea we've either hit a nerve or made a mistake. On more occasions than I can count I've chucked every plan I've had for a show in order to tap into a flaming phone bank.

I get paid for my instinct.

Chapter 8

"It was April the 41st. It being a quadruple leap year I was driving in downtown Atlantis. My Barracuda was in the shop, so I was in a rented Stingray, and it was overheating. So I pulled into a Shell station. They said I'd blown a seal. I said, "Fix the damned thing and keep my personal life out of it, OK, pal?"

"Wet Dream"
Kip Adotta

It's the biggest story in the radio business...since the last time it's been the biggest story in the radio business. The Federal Communications Commission, enthusiastically encouraged by nervous politicians looking for an easy mark during an election year, have started another indecency crackdown on the radio industry.

Nobody can dispute the fact that language in this country has experienced a general "loosening" since the late '80s when the government, led by what we called "Ed Meese and His Mind Police," began fining the biggest morning shows on the nation's biggest radio stations. While at KSD, you'll recall we were on the receiving end of a $2,000 slap on the wrist for reading parts of what was, at the time, the yet-to-be-released *Playboy Magazine* interview with Jessica Hahn. That piece would lead to the downfall of Jim Bakker and *The PTL Club* and a complete reexamination of the entire televangelism industry. I'll go to my grave defending my choice of having read the segment the FCC ruled objectionable, for it contained no profanity and — especially since it was read from an advance copy of the publication — clearly constituted a legitimate news story. In fact, it could be argued it was the biggest scandal, if not the biggest news story, of that entire year.

But it was because of the complaint of one person, a woman from Ballwin, Missouri, that the FCC felt it had reason enough to save St. Louis from *J.C. and The Breakfast Club* because we had "violated community standards." No widespread, public outcry. One person. How were they sure the woman was even mentally stable and not one of those people you see mumbling to themselves on a park bench? Apparently the fact that St. Louis has tolerated me and my act for the past 20 years and repeatedly made us number one in our time slot wasn't enough proof for the FCC as to what the community's standards are.

The government wants you to believe it's not the giant broadcast corporations that own radio stations but the government itself. The government wants you to believe they issue broadcast licenses that, in essence, "lease" individual radio stations to those corporations and owners. How pious the government seems when it insists station owners must prove they are operating "in the public interest," "for the good of the region" and "to serve the community." Then, the overwhelming majority of radio stations get away with airing one interview on Sunday morning at 4 a.m. with two old ladies running a bake sale to benefit the blind. The remaining 167 hours a week they present suggestive or even blatantly vulgar hip-hop, while making money hand-over-fist airing 20 minutes of commercials an hour. Right. "In the public interest."

The individual owners don't *own* their radio stations? All I know is if you can sell something it means you own it. And radio stations are bought and sold every day in this country.

On February 1, 2004, Justin Timberlake exposed Janet Jackson's right breast during the now-famous "wardrobe malfunction" at the Super Bowl half-time show. In what has to be the greatest example of absence of logic since someone decided to wage war against Iraq's leader in response to being attacked by a guy in Afghanistan, this country's politicians launched a full-frontal assault on the radio industry, raising indecency fines from the $20,000 range to the quarter-million-dollar range. The legislation so frightened station owners that the entire industry practically came to a stop for a period of several months in early 2004 while frantic corporate attorneys hopped from city to city scaring the pants off unsuspecting disc jockeys who thought this was probably just another indecency scare.

It wasn't.

This time it was the disc jockeys themselves who were being told their careers were at stake. "Zero-tolerance" policies began popping up on corporate-looking documents the on-air people were forced to sign, with clauses insisting the financial liability would be "shared." Did we understand this correctly? Should only one person complain to the FCC about something that was said on the air, perhaps even retroactive to the new, government crackdown, and should the FCC conclude what was said was "indecent," the radio host in question would be fired immediately, without any sort of due process, appeal procedure or legal recourse, and that radio host would also be expected to come up with an unspecified share of a quarter-million-dollar fine!

Yup.

Of course, this kind of talk is crazy, and our elected officials would never really follow through with such a thing, right?

Of course they didn't. They decided a quarter-million-dollar fine *wasn't high enough*. They raised the fine to a *half*-million. And they voted for it the same week the vice-president of the United States uttered the f-word on the Senate floor. Oh...the irony.

Clear Channel, the company that recruited, hired, promoted, oftentimes syndicated, and handsomely paid Howard Stern wannabes from one end of the country to the other for years, pulled the real Stern from a half-dozen of its radio stations, then attempted to portray itself as the guiding light within the radio industry while cutting what was considered a sweet deal with the FCC to avoid further scrutiny and big fines.

And even though it was an event on *television* that started the hysteria, TV just skipped along, almost without missing a beat. Pressured for the better part of a year by pompous organizations with names like the "Christian Parents Council for Family Values" and the "Commission to Put Pants on Donald Duck," the FCC finally fined CBS' affiliates an amount totaling less than one-third of what it costs to buy one commercial during the Super Bowl — about $550,000. But government threats? No.

Does anybody care how much blatant sexual content is televised on soap operas each week? Do the FCC commissioners ever catch "Springer," "Maury," or even "Entertainment Tonight's" obligatory exposé of the porn industry during every ratings sweep?

And then there's *Oprah*.

Don't get me wrong. There's no denying Oprah Winfrey's popularity and, if nothing else, the production values her show displays are top flight. Plus, she's the living, breathing embodiment of *the* American Dream. She provides a vital service, too. Where would women go for a daily affirmation that men are evil if not for Oprah? Even after having to sit through all three hours of *Beloved*, I have nothing against Oprah. However, why does Oprah get to giggle her way through sex quizzes, have almost weekly discussions of sexual dysfunction, or charge up an audience full of women with titillating details of the man who "woke up from surgery...*without his penis*"? Why should Oprah get to have all the fun? And why is it that the only people who ever have taken issue with her are a bunch of Texas cattlemen? Does the FCC view her show as "news," and thus allow it a free pass? If so, how does the FCC explain the fact that most of the rest of Oprah's shows seem to be about Brad Pitt or tips on buying shoes? Maybe the mostly male FCC commissioners are afraid their wives would make them sleep on the couch for a month if they ever messed with Oprah.

The fact that a televised event completely unrelated to the radio business has led to the most-chilling development in industry history while the medium responsible for the event continues with business as usual illustrates how defenseless radio is. It also proves what I've been harping on for years. Radio needs a Jack Valenti.

In the 1960s, Hollywood was facing many similar charges of indecency, particularly when films like *Blow Up* raised the ire of religious and political leaders. But Hollywood was smart. Hollywood knew it needed someone to act as a buffer between the vitriolic few, but influential, moralists and increasingly risk-taking producers and directors. That person would have to be someone with great mediating skills, a person both sides of the issue would respect.

Jack Valenti was best known as the dazzlingly well-connected advisor to President Lyndon B. Johnson. (In fact, you've seen him in the now-famous photo of the swearing-in ceremony aboard Air Force One in November of 1963.) For all of the film industry's faults — and there are many — for the most part Jack Valenti has successfully kept Congress out of the moviemaking business and, perhaps more importantly, out of the movie censoring business for the past 40 years. Valenti, a liberal, has convinced conservatives Hollywood is capable of policing itself while convincing filmmakers the downside of boneheaded decisions made by the Motion Picture Association of America rating board is far outweighed by the upside of a politician-less movie industry.

I hate the MPAA. I hate their double standard that punishes a director for a graphic love scene while allowing almost unlimited amounts of graphic violence. I hate the fact they've repeatedly missed the boat on establishing a rating system that would allow for an "adult" movie category that doesn't actually mean pornography. I hate their capricious attitude. But as long as American politicians continue to either fear or be a party to the puritanical demands of the religious right, the MPAA, even with its warts, is a necessity.

Should the radio industry figure out it needs its own Jack Valenti, I might hate the appointee. As was the case in 1960s Hollywood, it would take some getting used to having one man or woman telling program hosts, including myself, what the new boundaries are. But almost anything would be better than what the broadcasting industry has now — which is nothing.

As I argued on the *Sally Jessy Raphael Show* in 1988, once you begin censoring you immediately find yourself on a very slippery slope. What about the old standard, "She'll Be Comin' 'Round the Mountain When She Comes?" At Christmas, would someone find the lyric "Don we now our gay apparel" suggestive? Hell, a non-baseball fan might hear us talking about "pooh holes" and find that offensive. Recently, I was alerted to a Web site that shows before-and-after photos of celebrities who may have had plastic surgery. However, I wasn't able to access the site at the radio station since our company installed an Internet filter. When I pulled up the site on my computer at home, I didn't find anything I could have imagined obscene or indecent. There was no nudity...nothing! Just a noticeable increase in actress Tara Reid's cleavage.

The problem with all censorship is the same as it's always been: *who decides* what's obscene or indecent? Howard Stern is a riot to millions of his fans. His show is considered obscene to others. Personally, I find Rush Limbaugh's ridiculing of disadvantaged Americans, talk-show host Michael Savage's antagonizing of gays, and radio host Laura Ingraham's systematic looseness with the truth far more offensive than Howard talking trash to strippers.

When our company's corporate attorneys held a mandatory conference call/seminar for on-air talent in the wake of the FCC indecency ruling, we listened in as radio hosts throughout our nationwide chain of stations described bits they had done on the air in an effort to determine whether they had crossed the line. The questions covered everything from your standard dick joke to farting sound effects. When it was our turn in St. Louis, I described one of the most-popular segments.

I'd suggested on the air we help Jennifer Sparks purchase the building next to Bar Italia, the popular restaurant in the Central West End. She looked at me like I was nuts until I explained my plan was to call the new place "Jen Italia." The phone lines lit up like a Christmas tree. "Can I come inside Jen Italia?" "Is it true Jen Italia is closed one week every month?" "Can I get a box lunch at Jen Italia?" "I hear they have great finger-food!" "I'd like to eat there. Is there an opening?" "Rumor is their service is lickety-split!"

Of course, the whole thing was comprised of a skillful double entendre and there was no profanity uttered whatsoever. It's an example of how we — and hundreds of morning shows across the fruited plains — have been operating within both FCC and community standard guidelines for years. Our audience called to hear a replay of the bit nonstop over the course of the next few months. Two of our listeners asked if they could *buy* a copy. But, alas, our corporate attorney brought the hammer down. It hasn't aired since.

In 2003, a couple of Internet goofs in San Francisco got a ton of national press when they announced the first-ever "Masturbate-A-Thon." Apparently hundreds of people from all walks of life took part in the stunt which prompted me to ask: "What if you gave a Masturbate-A-Thon and nobody came?"

As funny as it was, you'll never hear that bit on the air again.

The double entendre has always been a staple of American entertainment going as far back as Mae West and continuing through the best days of *The Tonight Show with Johnny Carson*. Who can forget Art Fern's relentless firing on the "matinee lady" during Johnny's "Tea Time Movie" sketches? In recent years the double entendre has become far less sublime as the list of unacceptables has become shorter and shorter. Now we were being told even carefully executed double entendres were off limits. But, if nothing else, we knew where the line was. At least we did for 24 hours.

The day following the FCC ruling, the restaurant chain Houlihan's introduced a flight of radio spots with a naughty theme that seemed to completely contradict everything we'd just been told. The actors in the commercials portrayed a male restaurant manager instructing his female Houlihan's employees not to make fun of their "nooner" menu for fear of charges of sexual harassment. The women in the commercial begin to giggle as they trap their boss into admitting "in and out is good," and it's all right if you like it "fast and hot."

It was *precisely* what we were told we couldn't do anymore. Do you think money had anything to do with it?

For more than 30 years classic rock stations around the world have been playing Pink Floyd's "Money" and "Who Are You" by The Who, both with crystal clear profane utterances. Rap and hip-hop stations play songs every day with such blatantly obscene lyrics that it's almost laughable. How odd that we can *play* it but we can't *say* it.

Anybody who has ever spent any time in Europe knows how uncensored media is on that side of the world. It's not the least bit uncommon for an over-the-air television station to air a commercial or late-night television show containing nudity, for example. I don't see anthropologists lining up to predict the imminent fall of their societies.

Of course, I'm not advocating radio discontinue all semblance of decorum. But these periodic obscenity flare-ups and, especially, legislative activity are bad for everyone and always result in ridiculous, tail-chasing arguments that end up going nowhere. It never fails. Invariably an overstuffed congressman up for reelection will deliver the standard speech about "protecting the children." Did you ever listen to the way kids talk to one another at the malls on a Friday night? Does anybody really think they picked it up from Howard Stern? We talked that way 40 years ago when I was in grade school, and the disc jockeys I listened to on WLS in Chicago couldn't even say the word "pregnant."

In early 2004, following the FCC's indecency tirade, poll results were released indicating three-quarters of those surveyed were quite happy with the way their favorite, local, morning radio shows operated and indicated they wanted the government to stay out. It's further proof communities don't need or want an appointed body of bureaucrats in Washington imposing their entertainment tastes on us and that the members of those communities already know what their "standards" are. Religious groups, desperate politicians, and moralists need to STFO. They're never happy unless they're successfully dictating how the rest of us should live our lives. Do your thing. Let us do ours.

Chapter 9

"You and I have memories longer than the road that stretches out ahead."
"Two of Us"
Beatles

It was October of 2002, and the station had U-Man and me booked into a less-than-luxurious hotel in a less-than-luxurious corner of downtown San Francisco to cover the Cardinals' league championship series with the Giants. Apparently these were the best accommodations we could get. Either that or someone decided to try and save some money. All I remember is having to do all my recording, dubbing, and editing in the bathroom because it was the only place in the room with a grounded, three-pronged electrical outlet for my audio computer. Jet-lagged and tired from a full day of travel, John and I had a few drinks with dinner and knocked off. The next morning when I flipped on the TV for the local news I caught part of a story about a car that had gone out of control, jumped the curb, crashed through a giant plate-glass window, and ended up in the lobby of a building. "Welcome to San Francisco," I thought.

John and I met in the lobby fairly early that morning since it would be our only opportunity to do a little sight-seeing. I noticed he appeared a bit bleary-eyed, and he noticed that I looked the same. We traded stories of being awakened several times in the middle of the night from what seemed like the nonstop sound of sirens. We wondered what the hell kind of neighborhood they had stuck us in. As we pulled around the corner it became clear as to why we'd both heard sirens all night. To our absolute shock and surprise, there was the car we'd seen on the news, with nothing visible but its back bumper and tail lights...sticking out of the lobby restaurant of *our* hotel.

The truth is that this business seems to generate some of the weirdest stories I've ever heard. Some of what happens is by sheer happenstance, but I think a lot of it comes about because of the kind of people broadcasting attracts. In any form of show business you have to do outlandish things to get noticed, particularly when you're new to a city or just starting out. But just as often the reason we have so many odd stories to tell is because radio offers grown adults the opportunity to carry on as though they were still in high school.

Make that junior high!

One of the most awful chapters of my career occurred in 1976 when I was sentenced to a three-month stint at WTRX in Flint, Michigan. Miserable radio station, terrible facility, pathetic city, low pay...you name it. This was the station that was forced to eject its general manager when it was learned he had knocked up a very rotund, part-time commercial voice-over woman, then skimmed an unspecified amount of cash from the station to secretly pay for her abortion which, of course, he explained he had to do so his wife wouldn't find out about it.

The WTRX on-air studio was a dark, dingy place. I suppose that's why I got the idea one day to hide underneath the control board and wait for midday host Dave Barber to return from the men's room. I waited through two whole songs, just enough time for him to become very comfortable and relaxed back in his chair. The format required all of us to dramatically announce the call letters as the first thing out of our mouths following every song. The studio monitors muted as I heard Dave click the microphone on. He got as far as the "W-T" when I took both hands and clamped them as hard as I could around his calf from under the console.

"W-T-aaaaauuuuuughhhhhhhhhhhhhhhhhhhhh!!!!!!!!!!!!!!" is what listeners to the Dave Barber show heard that morning. I can't tell you what I heard from the program director a few minutes later. But it's rare that you get to hear what all-encompassing terror sounds like coming from a fully grown adult male.

Following my departure in 1986, KSHE was on about their fourth attempt at constructing a morning show to go up against us at KSD. This time it was a Vegas import who simply went by the name "Byrd" that was paired with U-Man. He was slight of build, and his long blonde hair reminded a lot of people of the '80s pop duo, Nelson. The station ended up broadcasting from an area McDonald's one morning, promoting a "score-a-goal, get-a-free-burger" deal. What Byrd didn't realize, though, was that they were expecting him to don full goalie equipment while wild-eyed listeners using real hockey sticks were to fire real pucks at him. At show time, Byrd, possessing little athletic ability, wanted no part of the idea. That disappointed and even angered some listeners who had gone out of their way to attend.

One of the station's young technician interns was on hand to pick up a few pointers on how to properly engineer a remote broadcast. Being a hockey enthusiast and watching what was happening, he shoved an elbow pad down into the crotch area of his pants, suited up, and got in goal. For several minutes he turned away shot after shot to the delight of the crowd. It was all going just a little too well.

Writhing in pain, the intern was helped into the restaurant bathroom following the errant slapshot that hit him...well...in the "McNuggets." Upon close, self-examination, he reported one testicle had swollen to almost twice its normal size. To this day, we're not sure whether the emergency surgery was necessary to repair a tear, an "explosion," or just a direct hit. We all understand why he's still not very forthcoming about the details.

Byrd struck again awhile later when a newspaper article describing the psycho organization, People for the Ethical Treatment of Animals, successfully halted construction of a highway when it was discovered a burrow of rabbits was being displaced. The next day, Byrd and U-Man announced plans for a live broadcast during which they would allow a rabbit to cross the street during morning rush hour near the intersection of Grand and Arsenal. As you might expect, officials from PETA lost what was left of their collective minds, trying unsuccessfully to get the spectacle stopped.

On the morning of the event, PETA and other animal rights protesters lined the street displaying banners and placards expressing their outrage. A caged rabbit was on display in the window of the restaurant-bar as the countdown began. Odds were projected. Bets were placed. The time had come. U-Man ceremoniously removed the rabbit from its cage. It was at that moment Byrd emerged from the building wearing a bunny costume he'd rented the night before. He strolled leisurely across the intersection as KSHE fans roared with laughter. Oddly, this seemed to anger the PETA people even more.

While this makes a hilarious radio story, it also makes you wonder why the kid didn't catch on in St. Louis. But we had hit full stride at KSD with our enormously popular show at the time which made it nearly impossible for him to get a toehold. It's a sobering reminder of just how long it takes and how difficult it is to build an audience when you're the new guy in town and that periodic stunts only get you so far.

In 1979, a struggling radio station that I'd been hired by a friend to try and fix decided a few TV commercials might help turn things around. Since one of our calling cards was the fact we carried the Grand Rapids Owls hockey games, the script called for me to deliver some lines from center-ice of the local rink. Owls star Guido Tinisi (who appeared in the Paul Newman classic film, *Slap Shot*) was to quickly skate up to me and hit the brakes, which would produce a spray of ice shavings. As is the case when filming a commercial, we anticipated shooting at least 20 takes. But on the fifth take, unbeknownst to me, my boss had instructed the hockey star not to stop, but to knock me over. You know. Just for "laughs" and for an outtake, perhaps to show at the company Christmas party.

Unfortunately, when you tell a cement-head, minor-league hockey player to "knock him down," apparently he thinks it means you want him knocked down like it's *freakin' game conditions!*

I never knew what hit me. More than a dozen trips to the emergency room and chiropractor over the next few years produced little relief. Neck surgeries in 1990 and 1995 finally corrected most of the problem.

Television produces its share of goofy stories, too. During the Rams' Super Bowl run in 2001, KMOV dedicated a few minutes on the early news for one of those hokey satellite hookups designed to create a sense of rivalry with the team's next opponent which, in this case, was Tampa Bay. The way these things usually work is that a reporter from the out-of-town city is told he'll be doing a live shot back to St. Louis, and just to talk some smack about how the Buccaneers are going to win and how their city is such a better place and blah, blah, blah. But live shots like that provide only audio for the reporter, not video. He can only hear but not see the people he's talking with in St. Louis. So, near the end of the piece, he bragged about how much nicer the Tampa weather was in January compared to St. Louis and concluded: "So when you come to Tampa, be sure you bring plenty of this," as he proudly displayed a bottle of suntan lotion to illustrate his point.

There was only one problem. He was speaking to KMOV anchors

Julius Hunter and Myriam Wright. I'm sure the reporter wondered why all he could hear in his earpiece was the sound of two *African-Americans* cackling hilariously.

Maybe this business produces so many weird stories because it attracts so many weird dudes. And some of the goofiest have been the people in charge.

You've probably heard us talk from time to time about "audition tapes." A radio host looking for a new job records an entire four-hour show, then edits out all but the parts in which he or she is talking on the air. What's left is a fast-paced, four or five-minute "audition tape." Radio people have been arguing since the days of Marconi about exactly what kinds of things on a tape will catch the ear of a PD. Getting through to the program director of a station you'd like to work at can be next to impossible, but if you're successful, and if you can get the PD to acquiesce to the point where he says those golden words, "Okay, send me a tape," that can be half the battle. It can also be a classic blow-off.

A PD at a prominent St. Louis radio station years ago was being hounded by a sort of strange guy with absolutely zero experience in broadcasting who wanted more than anything to get a job at his station. Movie screenings, concerts...every place this program director went the guy was there, begging him for his big break. One night, trapped at an event at which he couldn't shake the guy, just to get *rid* of him, the exasperated PD told him, "Okay, send me a tape." Those who were there that night recall a puzzled look on the guy's face. Remember, the dude had absolutely no experience in radio. Regardless, he scampered off like a 12-year-old whose mother just told him he could go see *Lord of the Rings* with his friends as soon as he made his bed. A few days later the PD was going through his mail and recognized the wannabe's name on a large, brown envelope. When he opened it he saw that, indeed, the guy had sent him a tape. He'd sent him a cassette copy of Pink Floyd's *Dark Side of the Moon*!

In my first book I detailed many of the run-ins I had with, arguably, one of the most-influential people in the city's history, former KMOX vice-president and General Manager Bob Hyland. It just cracks me up the way some people still refer to him as "Mr. Hyland," as though there's a chance he might rise from the dead and, using the "Voice of God" delivery he made famous delivering his weekly editorials, get in their face to demand continued reverence. While there are those, particularly amongst the old guard deep inside KMOX, who insist on perpetuating the borderline mythological status he enjoyed until his death over a decade ago, many more of us have known the real score on this guy for a long time and recognize him as one weird dude.

By now, almost everyone has heard the stories of his bizarre work schedule, most days arriving for work in the vicinity of 3 a.m. And you'll recall that in *Real Life Stories of JC and The Breakfast Club or Twenty Minutes in the Dark with Madonna*, I provided detailed accounts of his many overnight transgressions. But it's Hyland's squirrel-headedness that remains legendary in local broadcast circles. The broadcast chief was so obsessed with what he felt was television's increasingly negative impact on radio — not to mention his irritation over having to watch one employee after another use KMOX as a springboard into local TV news — that he instituted official station policy forbidding any discussion of TV on the air. (That policy would eventually be adopted by several other CBS news/talk stations around the country.) So in 1984 when Hyland gave the green light for his KHTR disc-jockeys to host a weekend, late-night music video program on KMOV called *Hot Hit Video*, a lot of media observers took notice. But he had given his approval with the proviso that the face of the talent never be shown on camera. All the viewers could see of the host was a lot of giant hats, odd lighting, and distant camera angles and reverse shots.

The general manager for most of my time at The River was the closest thing to a clown I've ever had as a boss. A large, clumsy, dopey-looking guy, he reminded me of that one kid we all knew in high school who was 6' 5", 230 pounds...but didn't play any sports. The first time I had to go somewhere with him in his car I realized what I was dealing with. As he drove me through the busy streets of downtown St. Louis I saw him begin fumbling for something under his seat. The next thing I knew he had rolled his window down and was yelling for the attention of a pretty pedestrian businesswoman while he held up a homemade cardboard sign that was affixed to what looked like a giant tongue depressor with the words "Nice Legs!!!" Not only did he seem quite proud of his creation, but he reached under his seat again to reveal a half-dozen similar signs, each with phrases like "Ooh La La" and "Sweet Stuff." Keep in mind we're talking about a fully grown married man in his forties, not Ralph

Malf or Potsie.

One day he was just gone. I never asked for details.

But of all the things I've seen in my nearly 30 years in electronic media, nothing even comes close to the unbridled insanity I witnessed over the past few years in the northeastern corner of the Union Station Powerhouse, home of the *Steve & DC Show*. In fact, had I not seen some of this stuff with my own two eyes I never would have believed it.

It had been years since I'd encountered Steve Shannon and D.C. Chymes, so when I arrived at the Emmis Broadcasting studios for my first day of work in 2002, I wondered what it would be like being in the same building and running into them everyday. But you might be surprised to learn that — although we worked on the other side of a piece of frosted glass from them for two whole years — I didn't even see them more than two dozen times. I was shocked at the sight of each having put on an enormous amount of weight, Steve particularly having ballooned out to such a gargantuan, unhealthy looking proportion that he seemed to sweat profusely even when standing still.

The pair never once attended a single staff meeting, official station function, party, or informal gathering in the entire two-year period so I can't claim, even now, to know them. But their presence in the building produced such a disproportionate degree of distraction and drain on company resources that I found it incredulous Emmis Broadcasting had been subjecting its other employees to this kind of nonsense. Each morning I'd arrive to a virtual free-for-all as up to a dozen producers, assistants, interns, boyfriends, girlfriends, family members, common-law spouses, hangers-on and other troll-like riff-raff wandered about making the place look like a cross between a cult compound and a white trash fraternity hazing rather than a professional broadcast facility housing five separate radio stations. It was obvious that personal appearance, personal hygiene and, for that matter, personality was not a high priority for this group. One young woman who had briefly served with them told me *Steve & DC Show* interns and their other support people were always firmly instructed not to speak to us. We were more than happy to grant their wish and exclude social contact with this tribe of social misfits, druids and other bacteria, while maintaining as much distance as possible from their unique brand of sewage that masqueraded as a daily radio show.

But it was the beginning of the end for the pair when ratings fell as low as 15th place while a series of devastating published local news reports detailed a personal lifestyle marred by excess combined with questionable financial and business dealings on the part of D.C. Chymes, aka Isaiah Wilhelm.

Late in 2003 Emmis Broadcasting announced it was pulling the *Steve & DC Show* from the local airwaves, though their show would continue to originate from our building until the duo could make other arrangements. On a few occasions Steve Shannon seemed to try and reach out to certain members of the staff, present company included, but it was a case of too little, too late. And though he seemed to possess at least some humanity, the systematic sleaziness of his radio operation continued. The brilliant *Mad TV* comedian, Frank Caliendo, confided in us that he'd never been paid for a series of celebrity impersonations that he provided their show on a weekly basis. One morning I overheard an older gentleman who was on a cell phone in a holding area for upcoming guests of their show. From the one side of the conversation I could hear I was able to ascertain that his wife couldn't seem to figure out why she couldn't pick up the *Steve & DC Show* at her home in St. Charles. "Tell her to listen on the Internet," one of their producers offered. "We have lousy reception in St. Charles County." This, of course, was completely duplicitous since the reason the woman couldn't hear the show was because they weren't on the air anymore in the St. Louis area.

Throughout this bizarre pageant I wondered if the night-and-day difference that existed between us and them was simply a by-product of a mostly cultural or generational divide. It wasn't. The awful truth is that a great philosophical chasm seems to have opened between the aging, socially conscious baby boomers in our business and the now fully mature Generation Xers. Ongoing, intense debate over the great moral and ethical questions like the ones we saw depicted in *Broadcast News* and *All the President's Men* aren't even on the radar screen anymore, let alone being discussed. When I got into the business in the '70s, talk radio stations were inhabited by people who had gone to college, had some formal news training, and demonstrated some level of knowledge of the world. Over the years, talk shows have begun popping up on the FM dial hosted by people with lots of opinions but without the credentials. And every day I notice people in broadcasting with a journalism background think *entirely* different than people who don't.

Finally, over the 2004 Labor Day weekend a team of knuckle-dragging grunts from the *Steve & DC Show* legions removed all but the last traces of the former number-one morning show from the Union Station Powerhouse. The grotesque nightmare for the people of Emmis was over. There was an immediate and dramatic decrease in the amount of whizzing on the toilet seats in the two men's rooms. Meanwhile, it took a detail of station staffers almost two weeks to scrape the crud from their suite of studios in order to prepare it for further use by humans.

Stories had been circulating for years suggesting the pair had anything but conventional lives prior to their arrival in St. Louis. Whether it was the intoxicating effects of money and success, an absence of parental instruction at an early age, or a combination of both, this was one of those cases you hear about in which two people watched their downfall occur at twice the speed of their meteoric rise. There are schools and classes that can teach you how to do almost anything — including radio. However, there is almost no substitute for a quality upbringing when it comes to preparing you for life.

Chapter 10

"Money changes everything."
"Money changes everything"
Prince

Can you think of any occupation with a name less enticing than "disc jockey?" Would you buy a used car from a disc jockey? Would you want your sister to marry one?

The truth is that the radio industry hasn't done much to help its image during the past few years. How many times have you enjoyed listening to some guy on the radio, only to see him in person or on TV and think to yourself, "Ugh!!!!"

It's okay. Really! I think the same thing. Too much of radio has perpetuated a stereotypical image of the overweight, poorly dressed, poorly educated, unshaven, mullet-headed oaf who talks dirty, pulls moronic stunts and is in radio because he'd never be allowed on television looking and acting that way. In turn, far too frequently that implied second-class status is reflected by the men and women who do this job. Every day I hear professional broadcasters refer to what they do as "going to work" or worst of all "pulling a shift." My God, people. You're supposed to be putting on a *show!*

And I'm not a "disc jockey," either. I don't put on silks and ride around a track on a thin slab of vinyl. For quite some time I've had a policy regarding interviews with the press. You can do the story on me if you use the term "radio personality" or "radio host. " Otherwise, I'm not interested. Some of my colleagues may have given up hope for some renewed dignity within our ranks. I haven't.

The media, particularly television, really picked up on the incredibly unflattering "shock jock" moniker about ten years ago, often applying it to just about any radio personality who didn't work at KMOX or KEZK. I've long believed that TV fell in love with the term simply because it rhymes, much the way they recently began pumping out "road rage" stories ad nauseum simply because of the catchy alliteration. Many advertising agencies have a blanket policy that states their clients are not to do business with stations that do shock radio. So it really does hurt us when that term is carelessly misapplied by dopey media types who aren't able to distinguish between Howard Stern getting gynecological with skanks off the street who think taking off their blouses will get them "discovered" and shows like ours that cut a wide path of discussion, entertainment talk, news, and jokes about everything from politics to kids' movies. "Shock radio" is a specific industry term for shows that tend to focus on issues from the waist down. Just because our show may shock you on occasion doesn't mean we do "shock radio." Hell, I've been shocked by things I hear on NPR!! And how ironic this sometimes careless, oftentimes deliberately dismissive attitude is by television, an industry that loves to tease us with promos promising that if we just stay with their newscast through the next two minutes of commercials, "the results of our special investigation may shock you!"

But in too many instances radio has become its own worst enemy. Much of our credibility has come at the expense of the short-term interests of radio sales departments. For years, I had to fight the knock that J.C. Corcoran was somehow "anti-sales." This, of course, is false and was usually the kind of stuff generated by unscrupulous sales people who got mad because I wouldn't let them push us around or erode the integrity of our show.

There may be no better illustration of my point than the case of "Body Solutions."

I'd had a lot of experience dealing with the high-pressure tactics of the diet industry in the 1980s when an outfit by the name of Nutri-System flooded the airwaves with commercials and hard-hitting testimonials by dozens of local radio personalities who claimed to have lost enormous amounts of weight by simply following the Nutri-System plan. The spots were so voluminous that it must have sounded as though Nutri-System had purchased the radio station. And I always thought it made it sound as though the entire radio industry was made up of a bunch of fat pigs willing to try any desperate measure to regain presentability.

Most of my colleagues couldn't resist the extra money that came along with the deal and, as you might expect, the sales department loved them for it. Knowing what I know about dieting and the diet business I wanted no part of it. We live during a time in which the diet industry, the sporting goods industry, and the health club industry all are booming — yet we're the most obese population in the history of civilization! Permanent weight loss can only occur as a result of a serious change in diet and lifestyle coupled with regular exercise. To suggest otherwise is lying.

For years I was approached monthly by the fine folks of Nutri-System and by our own sales people who just looked at me in disbelief over my refusal to acquiesce, or at least to take the money and sort of look the other way. Eventually Nutri-System, as was the case with so many diet crazes that preceded it, saw an empire crash. The golden goose had been cooked.

In the late '90s we began hearing amazing stories of a new, miracle product called "Body Shapers." I recall having a conversation with a then-KMOX sportscaster, Randy Karraker, who had been one of the first people on radio I'd heard claiming dramatic results... "27 pounds in just a few months!" Over the course of the next few years, nearly every well-known radio personality in St. Louis was hawking the product (which later changed its name to "Body Solutions") — each detailing the substantial weight loss he or she had experienced. Sales of the product boomed. Radio sales people raked in commissions. Radio personalities, encouraged by a series of bonus plans offered by the corporation, continued to pump out the inspirational testimonials. One fellow broadcaster showed me a year-end endorsement check for a whopping $22,000!

The live commercials all sounded the same. The copy read: "Just take a tablespoon of Body Solutions with a glass of water three hours after your last meal, and the weight will just fall off while you sleep while your body replaces it with lean muscle." But the whole thing sounded fishy to a lot of us. First of all, everyone knows if you eliminate late-night snacking you'll lose weight. So why would you need the dose of Body Solutions? Also, dieticians and doctors pointed to the fact there was nothing in the product's formula that was proven to have much of an effect on weight loss. Additionally, I noticed quite a number of the radio people endorsing the stuff weren't exactly what you'd call "svelte." And how in the world can you "build muscle" by sleeping?

The pressure to join the ranks of Body Solutions pitchmen was incredible, and the situation became more complicated when the company began sponsoring station events and promotions, and as Body Solutions became one of the broadcast giant's top clients. In fact, the KLOU 2002 Super Bowl broadcasts from New Orleans were underwritten by Body Solutions, and I was told I had to conduct an interview with the company's founder and president as part of the deal. As I wondered how I was going to dodge this one, the only two potential questions I was able to come up with were "How do you look at yourself in the mirror?" and "How can you sleep at night?" (By the way, I did manage to slide off the hook by having my cell phone turned off when the PR person called to set up the interview time.)

Finally, a series of exposés began to pop up in newspapers, magazines and television. Several attorneys general in various states around the country got interested. Though I still wonder why it took so long, more than five years after I'd first heard of "the miracle, evening weight loss formula," Body Solutions was no more. The entire outfit was finally seen for what it really was. The creator declared bankruptcy, cut a sweet deal with the government, and was fined a pittance. And in one of the great moments of poetic justice, radio stations around the country were left holding the bag for millions of dollars of unpaid bills.

On the day the government ruling was officially announced, St. Louis television crews scrambled to get local reaction from some of the dozens of radio personalities who had given listeners their personal testimonials. And now a shocker: a sudden outbreak of camera shyness swept through the local radio community. A couple of news outlets contacted me, mistakenly under the impression I had endorsed the product. When I let them know I hadn't, I was asked to appear in their stories. But the dirty little secret was already out. More than a handful of disc jockeys and radio personalities, from both AM and FM, will do almost anything for money.

I slept very well that night.

Even the older, AM radio crowd has gotten into the act. Recently a series of commercials featuring some of the AM band's most-familiar names began airing in St. Louis touting a new, miracle denture. What caught my ear was the fact that the radio personality didn't claim to use the denture himself, instead referring to "a close friend of mine." Plausible, right? Until I heard the identical copy with the same reference to "a close friend of mine" being read by another 60-plus, on-air talent from another AM station.

I was raised at a time when a person's word was the most treasured thing you could offer. To be fair, survival in the radio business requires the typical broadcaster to say and do lots of things we'd rather not say and do. Sometimes helping a struggling sales person by plugging a product or service about which you have little or no knowledge proves to be a more prudent choice. But nearly every company, restaurant, or business you've heard me do live endorsements for over the past 20 years is an outfit I patronize myself. Frankly, because people know me and recognize me on the street I'd be a fool to send you someplace I didn't have full confidence in. And in all fairness, the lure of an opportunity to make an extra $20,000 on the side when your yearly salary is only about double that probably would be terribly seductive. But, again, the men and women running the radio business are going to have to begin asking whether they can continue to give the tired old answer that "this is how it's always been done." The game has changed. Options like satellite radio not only remove commercials, they remove the *kind* of commercials we already know irritate people.

There's all kinds of pontificating I could do about sincerity in the broadcasting business, diminishing returns, and short-term benefits that would likely fall on deaf ears. Indeed...money changes everything.

Chapter 11

"One likes to believe in the freedom of music.
But glittering prizes and endless compromises
shatter the illusion of integrity."
"Spirit of Radio"
Rush

At least a half-dozen stations in St. Louis have engaged in the latest activity that results in a less-than-completely-honest outcome. The practice is called "group contesting."

When you hear your favorite radio station tell you to "listen tomorrow between 10 and 2 for your chance to win ten thousand dollars," it might be enough inducement for you to adjust your schedule and give it a shot. After all, 10 grand is 10 grand, and you have just as good a chance to win as anyone else in St. Louis, right?

Here's what they're not telling you, though it's more accurate to say here's what they *are* telling you that they know you're not catching.

Giant radio conglomerates with properties all over the country now possess the technology to conduct the same contest on all of their radio stations simultaneously. In other words, while you and thousands of other people in St. Louis are imagining what you're going to do with that 10 grand, thousands of listeners are experiencing that same fantasy in Houston...and Charlotte...and Grand Rapids...and San Francisco...and Seattle...and Orlando...and in cities all across the country.

Here's how it works.

A mass communiqué is sent to each of nearly one thousand stations that particular company owns all over the country indicating that, for example, Tuesday afternoon at precisely 1:06 p.m. Eastern, 12:06 Central, 11:06 Mountain and 10:06 Pacific Time, each station is to conduct the contest. Listeners then call, not the phone number of the radio station in their city, but a nationwide, toll-free number. When a winner is chosen from what is likely millions of calls from around the country, a recording of the lucky listener's excited reaction is MP3'd back to all the stations where it's played on the air. What you hear in St. Louis sounds just like every other radio contest you've ever heard on the air. But listeners are hearing that same contest across the nation...and nobody ever tells you the person who won the dough was listening to a station, say, in Portland.

The companies staging "group contesting" defend the practice by pointing out that by lumping that many stations together at once they can afford such enormous sums of money in the jackpot, something that would be impossible on a local level. They'll tell you the concept is no different from the sort of national contests done at, for example, McDonald's. And they'll tell you that during the contest they clearly state they're awarding the prize to the 95th "nationwide" caller. But the truth is that disclaimer flies by pretty quickly for most listeners, and almost nobody in the individual cities listening to their favorite station has any idea they're up against the entire country and that they have so little chance of winning. My guess is they'd feel duped if they knew. And if that's the case, what good has that broadcast company accomplished for itself?

The rise of technology has allowed some not-so-honest broadcasters to take further advantage of the listener. Digital broadcast lines allow KMOX swing-shift host Michael Dixon, who's actually based in Phoenix, to sound the same as any other St. Louis radio host. Not drawing attention to it is one thing. Opening his show with, "I'm looking out the window, and it's simply a beautiful afternoon in St. Louis" is something else.

Technology has again become the suspect with regard to the practice known as "voice-tracking." In theory, it was supposed to give a station in a smaller market the chance to have a big-city sound. It's done by offering a radio host the opportunity to pick up a few extra bucks each week by recording a daily show for a much smaller market. To explain the process I'll use St. Louis and Savannah, Georgia, as the example. A special software program is loaded into a computer in the St. Louis studio that allows the host of the show to hear the last 20 and the first 20 seconds of each song programmed for that day's airing at the Savannah station. One by one, the St. Louis host does his or her schtick over the tail end of each song and then introduces the next. The amount of supplemental information that's given to the host varies greatly, but it's fairly standard for someone in the receiving city to fax or e-mail weather forecasts and information about sports teams, community events and other data that will, in theory, make people listening to that show in Savannah feel as though that on-air personality knows their city like the back of his hand. An entire four-hour show can usually be voice-tracked in about an hour. Then, that personality will go on to host his own show in his home city while a computer fires off the recorded show hours later in another town, miles and miles away.

It didn't take long for the talent side of the radio business to figure out what was really happening. As the voice-tracking phenomenon began to spread throughout the industry, jobs were getting eliminated at a record pace while broadcast companies' costs were falling like a rock. After all, once the special system was set up you didn't even need a live human being in the room anymore. The computer did all the work. And if the Savannah station's midday show, for example, was being voice-tracked out of St. Louis, that meant there were no employee benefits to be paid in Savannah, and instead of cutting the host a $40,000 paycheck a year, the going rate for the voice-tracked show from out of town is more like $10,000 a year.

Ultimately it's the listeners who suffer. How much can someone sitting in a studio a thousand miles away really know about a city he may never even have visited? It only stands to reason that names of people, streets, and events were bound to get mispronounced, and since the voice-tracked show oftentimes was being recorded over six hours in advance of its airing, what about an important breaking news story or severe weather warning? Our industry's mantra "the immediacy of radio!" is being seriously undermined.

As insane an idea as this is, things got even crazier when I arrived at KLOU in 2001 and was told a news department at our company's headquarters in northern Kentucky would be supplying our news updates each morning. This meant that two guys sitting in a studio five hours away who may never have set foot in St. Louis would go to a fax machine each morning to retrieve a stack of wire copy, record it into a computer, then send it to our town, where another computer would fire it off every thirty minutes. The idea failed from day one. The mispronunciations became a comedy of errors as these two clowns flubbed their way through stories about "KINE-er" Plaza, "La-MAY" Ferry Road, "Gra-VOY" Avenue and Creve "CARE." As if to perpetuate the duplicity even further, they tagged each newscast with the promise to interrupt with "Breaking News at Once." Well, how in the hell would they have done *that*?

It took over a year-and-a-half of complaining about this daily nonsense before I could get "Dumb and Dumber" replaced with a local newscaster. Later I learned the whole concept had been cooked up by a corporate suit at Clear Channel for whom it would have caused great embarrassment had the "experiment" not been allowed to run its course. But that experiment came at our expense. Our newscasts carried less credibility than one of Les Nessman's at *WKRP in Cincinnati*.

The heresy that is voice-tracking has reached epidemic proportions since the practice was introduced a half-dozen years ago. Instead of its original design to afford smaller market stations a major-market sound with air talent beaming in from bigger cities, the concept has actually reversed to the point where KLOU's midday show is now voice-tracked by a guy in the much smaller city of Birmingham, Alabama! In order to save money, almost all of my former station's weekend programming is also voice-tracked, which, early in 2004, produced one of the goofiest results I've ever heard in all 30 years I've been in this business. Here's what happened.

Weekends are home to lots of radio station remote broadcasts from car dealers, shoe stores, cellular phone places, and the like. One particular Saturday a KLOU on-air personality had recorded the afternoon show, then headed off to an East Side casino for an appearance and remote broadcast. Listeners actually heard the following:

> "103.3 KLOU...that's Simon and Garfunkel on a solid gold weekend...let's send it out to Big Al Brock live at the Casino Queen!"
>
> "Thanks! It's a beautiful Saturday afternoon here on the boat."

Again...only one problem. The guy who had pre-recorded that afternoon show which included the live toss to Big Al Brock on the boat...was Big Al Brock! The man tossed it to *himself.*

The radio industry has found itself under tremendous financial strain over the past half-decade, a situation that was made even worse by the aftermath of 9-11 and the economic downturn. Streamlining, downsizing, and cost-cutting have become harsh realities in American business. But radio has to consider the long-term consequences of its short-term, quick fixes, or the industry runs the risk of crashing down the road toward a highly uncertain future.

Chapter 12

"Fifty-seven channels and nothin' on."
"Fifty-Seven Channels"
Bruce Springsteen

My first book, *Real Life Stories of JC and The Breakfast Club or Twenty Minutes in the Dark with Madonna* was almost exclusively dedicated to the business of radio. But after a cumulative 15 years logged at the two biggest TV newsrooms in St. Louis, and after watching more television over the past 50 years than anyone else I'm personally aware of, I may know more about television than I've been giving myself credit for. I've either lived in or traveled to dozens of cities in this country and others and always had an active interest in what was going on at the local TV stations. I travel with a small, portable, 8-mm VCR that's allowed me to collect samples of video from all over the world. I was an early DirecTV subscriber, and for several years I owned a ten-foot satellite dish with all those little magic descramblers and decoders you've heard about. Instead of using all of this technology to view multiple airings of *Jeopardy*, for years I pounded that remote until my fingers were blue, pulling down hundreds and hundreds of local and network channels along with a ton of closed-circuit feeds, live shots, and other private transmissions not intended to be seen by anyone outside television station "signal acquisition" centers. I once saw a few minutes of a satellite feed from the oval office in the White House during which an angry President Bill Clinton took the head off of an aide for not following through on a script change only moments before he was to address the nation regarding an American missile attack.

To this day, former TV critic Eric Mink and I marvel over the fact that I was able to eavesdrop on the entire KSDK newsroom one afternoon. Eric was instructed to arrive at their studios to be interviewed via satellite for a New York-based television show, and, as is generally the case, a live picture and audio were fed to the "bird" a half-hour early so that any technical glitches that might be present could be ironed out. From having spent so much time playing around with the dish in the past, I knew the satellite coordinates KSDK usually used and dialed it up. There it was. A live picture with audio from the Channel Five newsroom at four in the afternoon, one of the busiest times for a local newsroom. It was as if I was an invisible man. What made it even better was the fact I overheard an awkward exchange between Eric and then-KSDK reporter, Sarah Harlowe, who took the opportunity to blow him some crap about a column he'd written a few years back that was critical of her work. You can imagine Eric's response when I called him after the show and was practically able to repeat the exchange verbatim.

During that period from the mid to late '90s I watched Tom Brokaw get increasingly irritated with a makeup person, saw Dan Rather take forever to blow his nose, and listened to what used to go on in the broadcast booths of professional sports telecasts after they cut to commercial breaks. Whoa!

Local television clearly takes its cues from the big boys at the network and syndication level. Remember the "shaky, hand-held camera" video popularized by MTV in the '80s? Within months you couldn't go 10 minutes without seeing that technique used in local news and local commercials. As soon as a few nationally known news anchors were instructed to get out from behind their traditional-looking news desks, entire sets were being redesigned in newsrooms across the country to allow anchorpersons to move about the studio or stand to the side of enormous video screens to deliver the news. And walking became a big thing, too. The future suddenly turned bright for any anchor who could walk and talk at the same time. Again, this was something that began on the network level.

It seems like every generation has had its turn at predicting the demise of television as we know it. In 1961, then-FCC Commissioner Newton Minnow made his famous "television is a vast wasteland" speech and, in the best example of how closely FCC commissioner's speeches are valued, CBS debuted *The Beverly Hillbillies* a year later. The "jiggle TV" trend of the '70s gave us *Charlie's Angels* and *Three's Company*, while the '80s marked the beginning of America's gradual transition to cable with MTV and, for the first time for the medium, graphic nudity and previously outlawed language on HBO and other pay channels. By the '90s the explosion of inexpensive, audience participation talk shows like *Geraldo, Rikki Lake, Charles Perez* and *Morton Downey* had already experienced a rise and fall to the point where only a handful of the more than 50 new shows of its kind were still in production. Now, four years into a new century, it's "reality" TV and infomercials that litter the broadcast landscape.

As each of these new trends unfolded, television seemed to compromise its cultural significance a notch. Cable and satellite have morphed into an odd mix of "supercell," niche programming and B-level movies, counterbalanced by the brilliance of *The Sopranos* and *On the Record with Bob Costas*.

The change in America's entertainment appetite eventually had an impact on the networks' news divisions. Despite the fact that they may have been competent journalists, stuffy-looking newsmen in bad suits and horn-rimmed glasses with little on-camera presence were replaced by younger, more attractive men and, eventually women, with...*gasp*...sex appeal!

It was all part of the necessary evolution of the networks and the network news business. Change was inevitable. What seemed to go wrong is that the changes went too far, and as the money rolled in, anybody who suggested tapping the brakes in the long-term best interests of the industry's overall integrity was steamrolled. The next thing anyone knew, we turned on our TVs and half-naked people were eating bugs, and Dan Rather, Tom Brokaw, and Peter Jennings were doing stories about it on the evening news.

John Leonard, for years the self-inflated media critic on CBS' *Sunday Morning,* recently stepped out of semi-retirement for the show's 25th anniversary to offer an overwritten yet incisive commentary on the state of television in 2004. An excerpt:

> "Maybe we no longer need stories where intelligent action and moral purpose are made coherent.... Maybe words are guilty of association with rational comment, abstract ideas, the history of human thought, the library of human feelings, home truths, and collective memory. Nowadays, privileged at the computer and the plasma screen, looking down as if

> from elephants or zeppelins on a discourse of jingles, insults, slogans, clichés, brand names and bumper stickers with multiple views of Paris Hilton and in intimate focus and an I.V. feed of lewd data. Who wants a worrywart making distinctions? A spoilsport making connections or a storyteller making magic? We might as well just grunt and ogle."

There has been so much focus in recent years on network television – what with the shock value of "reality" shows and other spectacle – that local television, particularly local TV news, has been deteriorating right under our noses from city to city across the country.

Over the years I've spent an ungodly amount of time watching local news. With a lot of help from TiVo, on any given day I'll see one or two of the noon shows plus all three affiliates' early and late newscasts. Toss in the *CBS Evening News,* an occasional stop on one of the evening cable news programs and whatever I can catch out of the corner of my eye from the morning news shows while we're on the air, and my intake of news probably rivals that of any morning host in the city, including those on KMOX. If there's a big story taking place, that intake doubles. (I always laughed when callers or e-mailers, frustrated by my refusal to back George W. Bush's invasion of Iraq in 2003, insisted I was "uninformed." The fact was I'd most likely tripled them in raw numbers of hours in front of a satellite system, on the Internet, or in other ways of monitoring news.)

As for local news, I've seen it slowly decompose to the point where it's now become, on a good day, entertainment, and on a bad day, a parody of itself. I wish to make it clear that I have many friends in the local news business, and I find what's become a dwindling majority of them to be honest, proud, hardworking, legitimate journalists. However, as has been the case with most of the broadcasting world, understaffing, cutbacks, pressure, shareholders demands, deadlines, and downsizing have collided with apathy and ineptitude to produce a product that's a shell of what it used to be. Mistakes I couldn't have even gotten away with doing entertainment reporting five years ago now seem to go on unchecked. Grammatical errors, mispronunciations, and sloppy reporting have replaced the pursuit of solid journalism. "Arctic" is now "artic" and "asterisk" is now "astrick." There's even an occasional "expecially."

Oddly, while male anchors still manage a distinguished look, gone are most of the classy-looking women in conservative business attire. It's now all about sensationalism, glitz, and overdone hair and makeup to go with sexy wardrobes for female anchors. The "stand-up" — that portion of the pre-recorded story in which the reporter appears on-camera — has replaced writing as the focal point. High-powered and very expensive consulting firms drill news directors, producers, and air talent on newly discovered methods of "communication" — like how to look into the camera more authoritatively, how to walk and turn properly, and how to seem more sincere.

Two things caught my eye in a recent public broadcasting special focusing on the television consulting racket. A segment highlighting KSDK showed how an advisor was brought into St. Louis to make recommendations on how to improve the station's look in the face of an increased level of competition. After days of evaluating every aspect of the newsroom operation, he had the answer: custom cabinet makers! That's right. Custom cabinet makers were brought in to install a polished glass countertop on the anchor desk. Not more attention to developing stories. Not more reporters on the street. Not giving editors more time to assemble packaged reports. The consultant got paid to bring in a shiny piece of glass.

The other segment I noted involved a woman at the consultancy whose job it was to screen the hundreds of audition tapes that flood their offices every year. This chick was so over-the-top she reminded me of something Cheri Oteri of *Saturday Night Live* might have cooked up. One by one she opened the packages, removed the video cassettes, and slid them into her machine. As the image of a female anchor from a small market appeared on-screen, the woman began making audible grunts as she commented on her unattractiveness and unsophisticated wardrobe. Then, as a handsome Milwaukee anchorman's tape began rolling, the woman started cooing like a pre-teen at a Justin Timberlake backstage meet-and-greet. "Oh, my God, he's so pretty. He's beautiful!"

She never heard a word he said.

When I comment on the deteriorating state of St. Louis' local news content and delivery, it's not uncommon for people to remind me that I spent more than 15 years delivering entertainment reports, movie reviews, and celebrity interviews on channels 4 and 5. But for the most part, my segments came at a time in the business when the rest of TV news was still news! Now, celebrity and lifestyle stories are stacked right on top of one another, and it all comes at the expense of the delivery of actual, hard news. Stations now highlight and promote their puff pieces to the point of defining what their station's news *is.* Particularly during the all-important February, May and November "sweeps weeks," I can't tell the difference between the 5 o'clock news and *Entertainment Tonight* anymore. By the time you subtract the happy talk, commercials, teases for upcoming stories, clowning around with the weather and sports guys, plugs for the station's Web site, more promos, weather, kickers, and filler in the typical half-hour local newscast, viewers are left with about 12 minutes of actual news. You'd think that time would be used more judiciously. My observations and criticisms aren't about picking on people for individual mistakes. This is about policy.

In what smacks of a deal cut with the devil, KMOV now devotes a nightly segment to what amounts to a blatant, free commercial for *The Post-Dispatch*, plugging what "big stories" will be carried in the next days' edition. Aren't the city's daily newspaper and local TV stations supposed to be competitors? Shouldn't they be trying to scoop the hell out of one another? And what stories that constitute actual, hard news get bumped each night in order to accommodate this cozy little relationship?

KMOV runs a weekly piece during its 6 o'clock news titled "Do the Right Thing" which highlights an area youth who broke up a fight at school, dialed 911 at the first sign of a fire, or in some way demonstrated good judgment. That's wonderful. It also doesn't belong on the news. Of course, KMOV could run the piece as part of a commercial break, but that would necessitate their giving up precious revenue time. It's much more convenient to give up precious news time. Meanwhile, politicians are robbing us blind and getting away with it because local TV news operations have been told the way to get ratings is to veer away from traditional, hard news and to present more human interest stories, features, and video of squirrels water skiing.

But do we get what we deserve? From the perspective of slick, high-powered, fast-talking consultants, maybe we shouldn't be surprised they treat us as if this were Mayberry. To them, maybe we look like a community full of mullet-headed hillbillies looking for funnel cakes, a fireworks show, and a free bobble-head doll. Oh, and don't forget those lottery numbers! Is it possible this and other small and medium-sized, midwestern markets aren't taken particularly seriously? If puff pieces, eye candy, overly hyped, sensationalized video, and gimmickry didn't work, we'd get something else from our local news operations and the consultants who coach them.

I mentioned "gimmickry." For a long time, KMOV had the market cornered on silly, trendy schemes with the hope of wrestling viewers away from their formidable competitor, KSDK. A brief look back reveals enough birdbrained ideas to fill a "How *Not* To" book. Perhaps the most famous example of this misguidedness was the "24-Hour News Source" concoction. Every hour on the hour, day and night, viewers got a encapsulated, 30-second news update from a real, live person. Pretty good idea, right? Except for the fact that it was outrageously expensive to have an anchorperson on duty at all times, even when there was nothing newsworthy occurring, especially during the graveyard shift when TV newsrooms traditionally enjoy some down time. And since it's highly unlikely any new money had been appropriated for the project, some other aspect of the total news operation had to suffer. On top of it, KSDK almost immediately responded with a duplicate plan which sold sponsorships to its news updates, thus generating new revenue for the station. Both stations eventually gave up the fight and returned to business as usual.

KMOV's "Lightning Locator" was supposed to offer the latest technology available to keep us all from getting struck and killed. A year or two into my stint at KMOV I found the "Lightning Locator" sign that used to hang over then-meteorologist Mike Nelson's weather center stuffed behind some junk in a storage room and took it home.

Then there was "Compu-Score," which amounted to nothing more than a computer monitor angled precariously near the edge of Zip Rzeppa's sports anchor seat on the Channel 4 news set. In theory, were the Cardinals to score a game-winning run in the middle of Zip's 10 o'clock sportscast, "Compu-Score" would begin flashing, vibrating, dimming the studio lights, and emitting a radioactive ooze that would immediately cause him to interrupt the proceedings and update the score. Of course, anybody who's been in television ten minutes knows everyone on the news set wears a tiny earpiece through which the sports producer watching the game in the adjoining room can pass along that information instantly.

"Fly Thru Radar" was introduced in the mid-'90s at KMOV. It consisted of the already-existing radar we'd seen for years during weather segments and angled the color images in a sort of 3D manner to create a computer-generated sensation of...oh, forget it.

Except for instances in which CBS prime-time programming scored outrageously high ratings due to Olympic coverage or other high-profile events, Channel 5 has remained the news leader through the years. Moral of the story? Gimmicks can work, but not if the product you're attracting viewers to isn't better.

Local TV newsrooms continue to try and find ways to snag you, particularly during ratings sweeps, the two most-important of which come in May and November with secondary periods in February and July. In fact, on July 13, 2004, KMOV employed its attention-getting "breaking news" video graphic and theme music three separate times for three separate stories in one, 30-minute newscast. The first story involved a possible drowning in a residential area (complete with aerial video from the station's helicopter). The second, a suspicious package found on the Vegas strip. The third, a light truck off the road and into some water in Pontoon Beach. None, interestingly, was treated as a major story by the next day's *Post-Dispatch.* But for viewers watching Channel 4 that evening, it seemed as though they were witnessing one of the most eventful news days of the year when, in fact, they were unwitting victims of news executives who made a conscious decision to jack things up during a ratings period.

The "breaking news" kick local television has been on has already produced potential complications for those stations using it. A typical local station in a city the size of St. Louis might spend hundreds of thousands of dollars a year on focus groups and other forms of research. If a competitor's use of a new gimmick shows signs of catching on or signs that it's a liability, everyone will know about it pretty fast, and a strategy is put in motion to react. In the case of KMOV and Fox2's frequent use of the "breaking news" logo and music, researchers at KSDK discovered that many discriminating viewers immediately saw through it as a deliberate attempt to sensationalize their news. Upon learning this, KSDK produced a promo stating: "We'll never call something 'breaking news' when it isn't."

But if you think Channel 5 was taking an unusually risky, high road by refusing to play the hype game, consider this: the station began using a logo nearly identical to the Fox2's and KMOV's "breaking news" graphic that read: "Developing Story." By simply changing the words they could make their claim while continuing to play the game.

Consultants were responsible for cooking up the Channel 4 "Extra" campaign in 2003. "News 4...Where There's Always Something Extra," the promos read. Suddenly KMOV anchors and reporters insisted their stories contained "extra information" and to stay tuned for an "extra report." Nine times in one 30-minute newscast in the inaugural year of the campaign, viewers were either told "we wanted to know," or that the reporter in the next story did some "extra digging." Of course, these phrases mean *nothing*.

As early as the late 1960s, television stations began changing the way they marketed their news operations. Soon, almost every region in the country had either an "Action News" or "Eyewitness News" station and, again, these slogans meant nothing. In the mid '90s, KMOV began opening its newscasts with the slogan, "Live, local, and late-breaking," only to abandon it a year or so later. Alas, Fox2 began using the identical campaign in 2003, and recently KMOX radio adopted it, too. It's another example of how transient consultants have conned their way into the offices of general managers all over the country, popping open boxes of magic bullets and snake oil.

Local television's credibility gets stretched a little further each day, resulting in anomalies that are either depressing or amusing depending on your point of view. In the spring of 2004, police released surveillance videos to all local television stations, purportedly showing thieves using stolen credit cards at a Mid-County electronics store. The following day, when the suspects were apprehended, Fox2 and Channel 4 each claimed "one of our alert viewers" was responsible for making the identification that led to the arrest.

At Channel 5, a one-on-one interview with the Duchess of York, Sarah Ferguson, ran midway through the all-important February ratings sweeps. But Ms. Ferguson's appearance in St. Louis had actually occurred over a month earlier. Is it still news when the story is held back that long just so it can run during sweeps? The station repeated this policy on September 14, 2004, when the world's most-famous POW, Jessica Lynch, was in St.

Louis as part of a day-long motivational speakers tour. KSDK presented a 15-second sound bite from Lynch during its 6 o'clock news, tagged by a mention that the entire interview conducted by Karen Foss could be seen in *November*. Channel 5 promotes itself as the station "Where the News Comes First," but where, apparently, in certain cases it comes in two months.

An incident at KMOV during the presentation of a story about New York's 2000 senatorial campaign should have resulted in a suspension of its anchor, Larry Conners, but instead, ended up as just another question mark next to the station's claim of objectivity. In what became a very successful combination publicity stunt/straw poll, a small, upstate pizza parlor had given its patrons the option of having their order delivered in either a Hillary Clinton box or in a box bearing the image of her opponent, Rick Lazio. When Julius Hunter finished the story, which at the time indicated Clinton was enjoying a commanding lead, he tossed it back to his co-anchor, Larry Conners who sniveled, "I wonder if that was a baloney pizza?"

And all stations are now guilty of deliberately omitting key parts of various news stories as a method of driving viewers to their individual Web sites. These sites require you to wade through a sea of pop-up ads, then a series of nosy questions about everything from your hobbies to your family's estimated annual income before you can even get to the page you're looking for. And where that personal information eventually ends up is anybody's guess.

A long-running KMOV promo touting morning reporter Virginia Kerr included highlights of her daily stops at local radio shows. But the dee-jays at one of the radio shows depicted in the promo had been fired two months prior. I guess it didn't help them.

More often than not, local television news messes up because of good, old-fashioned sloppiness, lack of attention to detail and a failure to focus on how the viewers "use" the information they tune into newscasts for. No better example can be found than with TV weather persons. One particular Saturday morning in the spring of 2004 I watched a local weatherman devote at least 30 seconds of a two-and-a-half minute segment telling me what the weather was going to be the *following* Saturday, a week away, while rain he hadn't predicted was falling at my house!! Extended forecasts of even three or four days out are useless and almost always dead wrong. They are creations of consultants and marketing departments who want you to believe meteorologists possess that degree of accuracy. They don't.

And for all of the slickly produced promos stations run to get you to believe their weather team is the best, might KSDK want to rethink its priorities? After being bombarded with the old "when-severe-weather-strikes-turn-to-us-because-we're-ready-for-anything" routine, twice in an eight-week period during the summer of 2004, regular programming was interrupted for a severe weather update when the meteorologist who was on camera was wearing a microphone that either wasn't on or wasn't connected. In one case the *wrong* microphone was turned on as viewers heard one side of a telephone conversation weatherman Mike Roberts was having with a caller for 30 seconds. And could the severe weather "bug" with the highlighted counties in the corner of the screen get any bigger?! There's nothing like trying to watch a baseball game with the infield being eclipsed by half of the Louisiana Purchase.

Speaking of sports, a moniker like "Home of the Cards" or "Your Home for Blues Hockey" has traditionally been reserved for radio or TV stations that have purchased the very expensive, exclusive broadcast rights to the full schedule of games. How interesting, then, that Fox2 has aggressively promoted itself as "the Home of the Rams" when, in fact, they simply happen to be a Fox TV affiliate, the network that carries the NFC games, the conference to which the Rams belong. I guess Fox2 means it's "the Home of the Rams" except during preseason when KPLR carries the games, or on the Monday nights when ABC carries the games, or when the Rams play an AFC opponent and the games are on CBS, or on Sunday nights when ESPN has rights to any games in which the Rams appear. Other than that they're "*the* Home of The Rams," dagnabit!

Perhaps there's no better example of local TV news abandoning journalistic integrity and crossing the line into entertainment than at sports time. The landscape now seems to consist of guys who either take their segments entirely too seriously or hacks who look as though they're auditioning for something on Comedy Central. Upon watching one new local sportscaster for the first time, Bob Costas told me his teenaged son, Keith, remarked: "This guy looks like he went to ESPN school." Actually, I'm not certain some of them went to school at all.

Introducing a Martin Kilcoyne live shot from Chicago, Fox2 second-string sports anchor Rob Desir uttered the following (mind you, this is the best translation I was able to ascertain):

> "What's goin' on, S-T-L-ILL side? Welcome to another edition of Sports Final. I'm Rob Desir. Thanks for keepin' it locked.
>
> Five Redbirds will be representin' the STL in the mid-summer classic. My main man, fitty-grand, pots and pans, Marty Kilcoyne is representin' us in the CHI. What up, Marty-Mar?
>
> That's gonna do it for this edition of Sports Final. Wanna thank Bo Hart and Marty-Mar representin' us up in the CHI. STL-ILL side. I'm out. Peace. Two fingers."

HUH?!

The whole thing reminded me of the scene in *Airplane* in which actress Barbara Billingsley ("Beaver" Cleaver's mom) has to translate a jive conversation between two black passengers for a clueless, white flight attendant.

So much of what annoys viewers enough to actually put down their bowl of dip and change the channel is fairly non-consequential stuff. Sometimes it's much more than that.

On August 17, 2004, KMOV's Larry Conners teased a story going into the commercial break that read as follows:

> "The judge calls it a 'potential development.' Why he decided to send jurors home in the Scott Peterson murder trial."

After the break, this was the story:

> "There is a break for the jurors in the Scott Peterson murder trial. Today the judge is sending them home citing a potential development in the case. The judge's decision came after a 45-minute meeting with the lawyers."

In that same newscast, sportscaster Steve Savard was placed in the opening segment to deliver news that Mizzou's freshman quarterback was facing undisclosed juvenile charges in St. Louis family court. This was the exchange between Savard and Conners at the end of that story:

Savard: "As you can imagine, Mizzou coach Gary Pinkel is being bombarded with questions. His reaction coming up a little bit later in sports."

Connors: "All right. We'll look for that later in this newscast."

Twenty minutes later in the actual sports segment this was the follow-up:

"Mizzou head coach Gary Pinkel said he will not comment on the situation."

In both cases, KMOV deliberately led their viewers to believe key details involving two fairly sensational stories would be revealed if they would just stick with them through the newscast. In both cases, their viewers were deliberately misled and received no new information whatsoever. This sort of thing is normal fare for KMOV and business as usual for most of the local news scene.

Staffers assigned to write news teases for local television appear to believe we're all pretty stupid. On KMOV's August 31, 10 p.m. newscast a tease read as follows:

"President Clinton was here and he spoke to us.
Hear what he had to say."

The phrase "he spoke to *us*" clearly implied there was one-on-one contact involved, something that would have been considered unusual and a real feather in KMOV's cap had it been an exclusive. However, when the story aired after the commercial break viewers could see a half-dozen microphones in the president's face as it was obvious he was addressing a group of reporters, a practice known in the business as a "gang bang." Again, deliberately misleading.

Another example of the manufactured phoniness common in local TV news can be found when a reporter tells you they've "learned" something. On KSDK's early news August 20, 2004, Leisa Zigman dealt with the controversy over police departments' use of Tasers, sometimes known as stun guns, which incapacitate perpetrators via a 50,000-volt electrical charge. After an excellent setup to the story, the camera slowly zoomed in as Zigman appeared onscreen, and with a look of great concern she said, "And now, NewsChannel 5 has learned these guns are about to be made available to the general public." The implication was that her investigative team had uncovered something new and compelling. But the story had been bouncing around media outlets for several weeks. To say "NewsChannel 5 has learned..." was an obvious attempt at over-dramatizing the report.

Media observers and critics have been debating the issue of "ambush journalism" for decades. The technique put *60 Minutes* on the map in the 1970s. You know the scenario. The unsuspecting subject of an investigation is confronted by a camera crew as he's stumbling out of a three-martini lunch. Lots of incriminating questions about why the subject has been dodging the media and where the missing funds are result in a very guilty-looking fellow, not to mention incredibly compelling television. But CBS quickly recognized there were several downsides of the tactic plus a long list of ethical questions the network was exposing itself to. Then, as if *60 Minutes* needed any additional convincing, Geraldo Rivera began to employ the ambush interview regularly on another network. Consequently, producer Don Hewitt and the *60 Minutes* gang adopted a new policy of using the ambush only as a last resort.

Here in St. Louis, however, Fox2 apparently never took the hint. They've been working the ambush shuffle several times a week as a vehicle to elevate one of its reporters to the level of star.

Even in the world of investigative journalism, a reporter who maintains good sources and develops a knack for where to look and how to effectively tell a story shouldn't find himself in the position of needing to ambush business people and governmental officials on a nightly basis. Of course, perhaps it's more a want than a need. If the newsroom brass makes a conscious choice to operate in this fashion, then it's easy to draw the conclusion that all involved have figured out that it's a lot easier to exchange the *work* required to operate an investigative news unit for the ease of throwing on nothing more than sensationalized video of a reporter jumping out from behind the bushes. The reports always seem to convey an odd sense of pride in reminding us the reporter had been "repeatedly turned down for an on-camera interview." Normally, that would be viewed as a failure. But the fact that Fox2 seems to have made its reporter Elliott Davis the main focus of its "You Paid for It" segments — as opposed to the story itself — speaks volumes about what the station's true motivation is. Fox2's tactics clearly presume a suggestion of guilt on the part of the targeted individual and oftentimes give Davis, a seasoned broadcaster, such a distinct and unfair advantage over city employees, clerks, and private citizens — with little or no experience in front of a camera — that the whole thing becomes tantamount to good, old-fashioned bullying. This is not to say that the unit doesn't occasionally do good work. Any exposure of true fiscal waste on the part of government is worthy of airtime. But when it's the reporter instead of the victim getting the bulk of the attention in a consumer or investigative series, that's backwards.

Fox2 faces the unenviable task of having to fill a whopping 20 hours of local morning news each week. Understanding the magnitude of that challenge is the first step in understanding how some of the stuff you see ever gets on the air. Don't get me wrong. Morning goof Tim Ezell is a marvelously talented kid. I'm just not sure what his presence on the show has to do with the fact the program is, after all, promoted as news. Truth is, all of the morning "news" programs on television, local and national, are fairly questionable about which side of the line they want to be on when it comes to news from entertainment. And like most forms of media, it's too easy not to resist the temptation to turn things into pure spectacle. In fact, substituting "activity" for actual entertainment is one of my real pet peeves when it comes to morning television. It's even worse when those attempts fall flat. I once saw a reporter on a weekend live shot cut to more than a full minute of three people in a park tossing a Frisbee around. There's so little actually happening at 7 a.m. in a city the size of St. Louis that most of what you're going to see is filler.

Particularly when you're talking about morning programming there's so much distraction in people's lives that some "fluff" on these morning shows is understandable. A tall, hairy dude in a dress, a rotund guy flipping off a toupee, or a fabulous babe doing squats in a Speedo (as part of an "exercise" demonstration) may be the only sorts of things capable of grabbing attention against the cacophony of brushing, flushing, and screaming kids getting ready for school. Frankly, acquiescing to the idea that people are not hanging on your every word is one of the first things you have to deal with when you get into this business.

The "Peter Principle" is alive and well when it comes to morning television, too. Men and women trained as professional journalists who come up through the ranks, covering fires and city council meetings, and who steadily work their way to the network, do not necessarily make good program hosts. I find it astonishing that the networks will repeatedly grab a White House correspondent, Capitol Hill reporter, or political analyst, and slap him or her up on your screen with an expectation that he or she will have some level of proficiency in the art of conversation, ad libbing, or any of the other skills necessary to effectively function as host of a show like *Today* or *Good Morning America.* Watching some of these people attempt to show they have a personality and sense of humor is truly painful. Jokes that aren't funny and couches full of people laughing at them anyway are all too easy to find every morning on every channel. How many more times do we have to watch a White House correspondent for the network get plugged into one of these shows and be forced into having to pretend interest in the latest low-carb barbecue recipe before someone upstairs finally realizes this stuff doesn't work? Once in a while the chemistry happens, but for every Matt Lauer who can pull it off, there are a hundred Campbell Browns who can't. (Brown, incidentally, is sensational on the syndicated *Chris Matthews Show* primarily because she's there to talk about her forte, Capitol Hill politics.)

Of course, the theory can operate in reverse, too. There's a legendary story in broadcast circles about the out-of-town network executive attending the Super Bowl who flipped on his TV one morning and saw what he considered to be the most bubbly, cheerful, entertaining local morning show host he'd ever seen. She was immediately signed to a contract, brought to New York and installed as co-host of *The Weekend Today Show*...where she flopped miserably and was gone in a little more than a year.

It's a similar situation in radio. How many times have you heard about a guy coming to take over a morning show in St. Louis who'd had the number one program in Nashville, Wichita, or Oklahoma City — only to see him fail to catch on? I understand that the common perception of this kind of work is that it's easy and that anyone can probably do it. But the next time you're thinking that way, ask yourself why so many professionals still fail at it, and why so much of what you see and hear is so awful.

Can anybody do it? Sure. Anyone with above average communication and speaking skills, an outgoing sort of personality, and a armload of opinions can do this job. For a while. Mike Bush, arguably one of the most talented, outgoing, and successful media personalities in St. Louis, took over my old radio show at KSD in 1992. He lasted a total of two months. That is absolutely not a knock on Mike. It's just that there's an enormous difference between reading a script off a TelePrompTer and having to come up with something to say off the top of your head that's entertaining and somewhat original four hours a day, five days a week. Perhaps I'm biased, but I believe history shows the best communicators, whether they're politicians like Ronald Reagan or late night TV talk show hosts like Johnny Carson, have a background in radio.

Television ratings sweeps occur on both a national and local level four times a year, but the biggest, most-important periods take place for a month in May and a month in November. That's when the networks air their big-budget specials and series, sit-com cliffhangers, lesbian kisses, marriages between series characters and tearful farewells. The results of these two ratings sweeps determine how much sponsors will have to pay for commercials for the following half-year. Because so much money is riding on these results, it's turned into a free-for-all — with "anything goes" for local stations and their news operations, as well as the networks.

In the weeks leading up to the two main sweeps periods, it's not uncommon to hear talk around the newsroom that a particular reporter is working "on series." These are the usually overblown special reports that air during sweeps that warn us, as viewers, that everything is about to kill us. To be certain we get the point, eerie music often accompanies the story as the camera tilts to one side the way it did when "The Riddler" would show up in the old *Batman* television series.

Better not go outside because the air has harmful pollutants. Can't go to the playground with your kids since the wood chips contain dangerous chemicals, and the monkey bars are covered with lead paint. Be careful at the supermarket since the beef has *e. coli*, the chicken contains deadly bacteria, the seafood isn't fresh and the fruit is from...(gasp)...CHILE! If you think you're safe in your own back yard, think again, Chester. The wood in your deck was treated with arsenic, and the lawn treatment you paid an arm and a leg for to keep from having dandelions might kill your dog. The recording of a 911 call from a frantic mother who found her baby floating face down in the family pool will make you drain the damn thing immediately and stay in the house! No, wait! You have MOLD!! Your air ducts are disgusting, your toaster might have a factory defect that could burn the house down to the foundation, and we *all* know what's in our drinking water. You'd better just run! Get the baby, get in the car and get out, for God's sake! Oh, no! That's right. Three of every four car seats are installed improperly! And heaven forbid you should become injured and require surgery because you might burst into flames on the operating table (and, no, I didn't make that up...Fox2 aired that one recently). By the time the news is over, you're convinced that bottle of spray cleaner you thought was so "harmless" just might sprout a head with fangs and begin gnawing its way out from under your kitchen sink.

Local television news has figured out that by cultivating a culture of fear, viewers will determine that they need the news to protect them from danger. Brilliant? Sure. Morally bankrupt? Sure.

Oftentimes these series pieces are lifted from stations in other markets that claim success after airing them. Frequently at Fox2, an entire story is pirated from another city, which means the video, interviews, and issues depicted may have little to do with any problem or issue in St. Louis. Of course, no reference is made to the fact the whole piece is originating in another market. The local reporter's voice and image are simply edited into the piece and nobody is the wiser, though there's an obvious impression left with the viewer that the story was shot locally. Obviously they're not counting on viewers noticing the "Ralph's" supermarket sign in the background, a chain of stores found only in the western United States.

It is not an exaggeration to say that local TV news becomes a completely different animal during sweeps periods. The concerted effort to produce and promote series pieces means big chunks of time have already been taken out of your daily newscast before the opening theme even hits the air. The business has always engaged in this sort of stuff, but things have gotten way out of balance in recent years. And here's the real kicker: sometimes the series piece you're watching isn't even about the information in the story. Sometimes that piece is actually a vehicle news operations employ to elevate the stature of a particular reporter the station is promoting.

Because of the cost involved, reporters sent out of town for stories are under additional pressure to come back with something particularly juicy.

And when it comes to advertising those kinds of stories, whether it's a breakdown of communications or deliberate over-hyping, often what are called "high concept" promos have a tendency to dramatically overstate their case. KMOV's Donna Savarese was sent to California to interview Cards manager Tony LaRussa and family early in 2004. Throughout the day we saw a promo teasing the points that would be featured in the 10 p.m. story including "...the one big regret he has since coming to St. Louis." KMOV dedicated almost four minutes to the story, almost double the amount of time a reporter usually gets, and Savarese did a fine job. However, nowhere in the piece was there a single mention by her, LaRussa, or anyone else in his family about any "regret" he had.

Stations are fiercely guarded about the stories they plan to spring on us during sweeps weeks, and for good reason. The best example of why that concern is justified occurred a little over a decade ago when someone at KMOV surreptitiously discovered KSDK had arranged for its anchor, Deanne Lane, to be disguised as a homeless person and followed by a hidden camera as she chronicled life on the streets of St. Louis as part of a February sweeps series. Believing they could pull off a textbook pimp job, Channel 4 quickly threw a plan together for its own anchor, Larry Conners, to be featured in an identical piece. When the Channel 5 brass saw their competitor's promo hit the air one Friday night, Lane was summoned immediately and KSDK was forced to rush their project ahead a full two weeks. The result was *both* Conners and Lane ending up practically passing one another as each of their stations' hidden cameras rolled just a few days later.

Wanting to absorb the full impact of the experience, Lane actually spent all of her days and nights on the street, sleeping in Larry Rice's homeless shelter and divorcing herself from most of her normal world. Conners, on the other hand, returned home each night and slept in his own bed. The proof was in the pudding. Deanne Lane was presented multiple local Emmys for her series while the jury seemed to note the transparency of the KMOV effort. But the lesson was clear as series work from that point forward has developed under a shroud of secrecy. It's now also standard operating policy to hold back promos teasing a new series until the last possible moment, with the intent of making it too hard for a competing station to rush a copycat piece into production in time. It's also not uncommon for a competing station to try and slap something together anyhow in an effort to steal some of its competitor's thunder.

Did you ever try checking out the other news shows when the one you're watching goes to a commercial break, only to find they're all in a commercial break? Again, no coincidence. Those breaks and even the placement of certain segments and stories are strategically designed to take advantage of the methodology the TV ratings companies employ. Manipulating the viewers so that they stay tuned for a particular number of minutes at a particular time in the hour produces a higher total rating for the station.

Indeed, local television has always looked for its cues from the big boys, the producers and talent on the network and syndication level. And as those players on the national level have stretched the limits of what's acceptable to increasingly questionable levels, why should anyone be surprised when producers and talent on the local level emulate them? Recently *Entertainment Tonight*, whose executive producer, Linda Bell Blue, the absolutely darling proprietor for the defunct, celebrity-hostile tabloid show *Hard Copy,* ran teasers on all of its affiliated stations, including KMOV, touting their lead story that day: "It's wedding bells for Monica Lewinsky!!" Viewers tuned in that night expecting to hear who the "lucky" guy was that had asked America's most famous intern to be his bride. What they got instead was a lame story about Ms. Lewinsky attending the wedding of one of her close friends. It's easy to see where producers and news writers in local TV get their inspiration.

I often hear from parents looking for advice for their high school or college kids with aspirations of working in the television business. I normally tell them four things: first, try and talk them out of it. It's a very tough racket with extraordinarily long hours and low pay as they're trying to climb a very steep ladder. Two, if you can't talk them out of it, make sure they go to a good university that will give them lots of hands-on training. Three, major in journalism but double-major or get a minor in *marketing* because that's what the business is becoming more and more every day. And four, show up at the Tamm Avenue overpass when there's even the slightest threat of snow. Every newsroom sends its reporters there for live shots over Highway 40, and your kids can ask them questions.

It's important to note that the increasingly questionable direction of local television news is rarely a result of any decision made by the man or woman you see on your screen. As is the case with anything, there are varying degrees to which TV anchors and reporters have drunk the Kool-Aid. Station general managers hire out-of-town consultants who sell them on the idea that they can "fix" their stations. Big money exchanges hands, so the snake oil gets handed down to the newsroom, where it's the job of the news directors and producers to make sure the writers, anchors and reporters operate in lockstep while the promotion departments push the message hard. If you stopped a hundred people walking down Market Street and asked, "Who is St. Louis' 'First Family'?" you probably wouldn't be surprised to hear names like Busch, Danforth, or Slay. But, according to KSDK's promotion people, it's Art Holliday, Jennifer Blome, and Scott Connell, its morning news team. The station went so far as to commission a song that plays incessantly overnight and on weekends as filler.

Less than a decade ago, Channel 2 news was face down and dead in the water following a long series of atrocious decisions by its management team. Who can forget their elimination of the all-important 6 o'clock news in favor of *Geraldo*? Then there was the importation of four entirely new anchorpersons, including Lloyd Immel who, during a live-shot from a fire in south city, actually asked the fire department spokesperson: "Where are we right now?" Months after news anchor Iola Johnson hit the air, questions began to surface about a police pursuit she may or may not have been party to prior to her St. Louis arrival. If the nondescript Miles Muzio knew anything about captivating an audience during his weathercasts he certainly didn't show it here. And what stroll down St. Louis television memory lane would be complete without a mention of Stu Klitenic, whose frantic mannerisms during the sports segment more resembled a cop directing traffic? Fox2 News, as it is now known, even with all of its faults, has risen from the ashes to become a competitive force in the local TV news game.

KMOV recently lost St. Louis broadcast legend Julius Hunter but replaced him with one of the most poised, professional, smooth, personable, and easy-on-the-eyes anchors this town has ever seen, Vickie Newton. Silly gimmicks aside, "News 4 St. Louis" gets credit for refusing to be dethroned as the perennial number two news operation in town.

And, of course there's "NewsChannel 5." With Karen Foss, our town's closest thing to royalty at the helm, it has remained number one for 20-plus years and for most of the right reasons. However, the promotion of Mike Bush from sports to news anchor — though a great opportunity for my friend and former co-host — really illustrates how the news business has become more about popularity than traditional journalism. And remember what I've always said about how fast things can change in this business. KSDK is living that nightmare right now as it's watched its sports department go from absolute domination to second-class status almost overnight.

I love TV, and I love local TV news. But because I do, I hate to see it slowly being ruined. The television managers and consultants cook it up; the producers and talent serve it up; and almost nobody holds them accountable for their actions. *The Post-Dispatch's* television columnist rarely focuses on these issues, and *The St. Louis Journalism Review's* circulation isn't large enough to make any real impact. Local news is becoming less and less about the actual information itself and more and more about the industry's manipulation of the audience — getting you to watch and getting you to return. Once viewed as a noble profession, too much of the management pool and even some of the on-air talent have infected the business with a "just-get-it-done" and a "ratings-are-king" mentality. Once you abandon your essence, once you stop the goal of striving for a higher ideal, once you're no longer true to journalism's historic past, you've crossed a dangerous line.

Local TV newsrooms never miss an opportunity to take a swipe at their ugly stepsister, radio. On the rare occasions when TV decides to cover a radio station's charitable event, it's common for the story to describe it as having been sponsored by "a local radio station." But if someone on radio messes up and is implicated in some sort of scandal, you can bet your lucky stars the guy's name and call letters will find their way into the story. Maybe it's time local television news cleans up its own house.

Chapter 13

"Still crazy after all these years."
Paul Simon

For most people, Friday's arrival brings a sense of relief and a cheerful anticipation of weekend activities and relaxation. Welcome to radio. Today is Friday. Let's just say the next six days will be a test.

Between now and Wednesday I'll be involved in a live broadcast prior to tomorrow night's Sting concert, another live broadcast Monday from the grand opening of the new Clayton Krispy Kreme doughnut store and yet a third live broadcast Wednesday from Bellerive Country Club, site of the 2004 U.S. Senior Open Golf Tournament. The Monday and Wednesday shows have the additional complication of including live TV shots. Each special show will require its own set of meetings with the sales, promotion, and engineering departments — plus research, pre-recorded segments (industry term: "production'), and other miscellaneous preparation. All of this will occur as producer/co-host Laurie Mac and I continue planning and developing segments, interviews, trips, and contests for shows as much as six months down the road.

It's 10:30 a.m. on Friday. Laurie has already left for the weekend to visit her husband, who's appearing in a play somewhere in Iowa. As much as I need some help, I'd like for Laurie to recharge and spend some time with Alan even more. Maybe I'll even get more done working alone. The "96 Minutes to Sting" show is the first order of business, since it's happening in 30 hours. We've already acquired a copy of the show's set list, so the next step is to grab all the appropriate CDs I'll need to get an idea of what songs I'll want to feature. Carl "The Intern" Middleman strolls in with the Sting boxed set that includes some live tracks which will sound great on the special. Earlier in the week Carl found an old vinyl disc with a tremendous live version of "Roxanne." People have always called me a pack rat, but Carl is a close second. Usually if I don't have it, he does.

I'm multi-tasking big-time. While I'm preparing all of this Sting stuff I'm racking my brain, pouring over the Internet, and checking my files for any movie or TV clips that mention doughnuts. The only decent reference I can find is a line in the Bangles' song, "Walk Like an Egyptian."

"If you wanna find all the cops
they're hangin' out in the doughnut shops..."

That's really lame. There has to be more...somewhere!

Finally, at 2:30 p.m. I close up shop for the day. On the way home I stop at Blockbuster to check out the Kevin Costner film *Tin Cup* and Bill Murray's comedy *Caddyshack*. Tonight I'll dub audio from those movies, along with clips from *Animal House,* the *Three Stooges,* the *Beverly Hillbillies* and Tim Conway's *Dorf on Golf* video to use on Wednesday's show from Bellerive.

No, it's not a joke. I own nine VCRs, though two of them were recently decommissioned and replaced by three TiVo units, the life-altering invention of the century. Each of these machines is wired in such a way so I can dub sound bites onto digital audio tape, which I can bring into the small production deck I have in the office. There I can edit and copy sound into one of our special broadcast computers we move into the on-air studio each morning. I began accumulating audio clips almost 25 years ago. Over that time I've developed a sort of sixth sense for what to add to my archives. Those clips are then titled and indexed on my laptop. At this point, almost any imaginable topic, promo, or theme we might need, I probably have. Ken Wilson's play-by-play of Pete Rose's 3,000th hit? Got it. Dan Quayle misspelling "potato?" Got it. Jay Randolph's memorable clip, "The Cardinals, Jack, off to their best start in 20 years." Of course.

I have at least one sound bite about everything.

Everything but *doughnuts*!!!!

I figure something will come to me. I've got until Monday, right? I try to convince myself this isn't driving me crazy.

It's 5 o'clock Saturday afternoon, and before I head for UMB Bank Pavilion, I place a call to *Showgram* meteorologist Dave Murray to ask what in the hell is going on. The forecast said "Sunny with a high of 80 degrees." It's rainy and cold. "Dave?"

Instructed to call back in an hour for a last-minute, updated forecast, I arrive in Maryland Heights about 20 minutes before we're to begin our show. The specially equipped K-HITS van sits just inside the main gate, 30-foot-tall mast pointed skyward, enabling our microwave signal to fly across town all the way to our receiver at Union Station. Three members of our staff are wet, cold, and holding onto our tent for dear life. Wind now, too? It's freaking *July!* It's 6 o'clock and the gates at UMB open. An old *Saturday Night Live* sketch with Rob Schneider as "the copy man" opens our show. "Sting...Sting-atola...the Stingmeister...der Stingelhoffer...Sting!"

Carl "The Intern" hears me count backwards from 5 to 1. We're on the air.

No, we're *not!*

An unforeseen technical malfunction produces a combination of hum and distortion that makes me sound like one of those dudes they interview on *Dateline* where they only show a silhouette and camouflage the voice. The first 40 minutes of this special show I worked on for five hours ends up being done over a cell phone. There's no one to yell at. Everybody's cold and wet and trying their best to fix the problem. I yell anyhow.

Thank goodness we end on the upbeat. Some poor guy and his wife will watch tonight's concert from the first row instead of from the muddy lawn as a result of our special drawing. The rain has picked up. Dave says it will continue on and off throughout the evening. By the time the show starts I don't even care anymore.

It's Sunday, and instead of spending the afternoon watching the Cardinals beat Barry Bonds and the Giants I'm at work. This doughnut thing is driving me nuts. Laurie calls from her cell phone on the way back from Iowa with a great idea for tomorrow's show from Krispy Kreme. We immediately begin developing questions for what we'll call "The 20,000 Doughnut Pyramid," a parody of the old Dick Clark game show. Writing all of the questions and preparing the game will take the rest of the evening. Normally the alarm goes off around 4:15 a.m., but since I have to drive all the way downtown, do all the regular preparation for the show, then drive all the way back to Clayton, that wake-up time gets moved up to 3:15. I make the mistake of turning the bedroom TV on as I get ready to knock off. Within 30 seconds I am hopelessly engrossed in the Independent Film Channel's presentation of *Pulp Fiction.*

I'm up after only three-and-a-half hours of sleep. Basically the feeling is indescribable, but let's just say it's even worse than I imagined it would be while I was watching the movie. I'm at the station before I know it, armed with a bag of equipment containing headphones, music, and commercial logs, two Walkman radios (one might not work and then what?), a bullhorn, Hi-Liters, a hand-held TV, a table clock and other assorted stuff I think I might need. All I have to do is pull the Game Show Network CD with the "$20,000 Pyramid" music on it, and I'll be on my way to Clayton. It's 5:10 a.m.

I've looked everywhere. I've checked and double-checked. I've interrogated innocent people in the hallways. The CD is missing. I'm incredibly pissed because I don't *lose* things. I'm certain someone lifted it. It's 5:30, we're on the air with the "replay" segment in 20 minutes, and I'm still at Union Station. I've got no choice.

I arrive at Krispy Kreme at 5:50 to some surprised looks. I'm sure most everyone thinks I decided to just cruise in a few moments before airtime. They have no idea I've been working on this show since Friday and that I've already been up for three hours. Channel 4's cameraman is wiring me up for our first live shot at 6:15. Jennifer Sparks is getting traffic updates over her cell phone. U-Man is looking over his first newscast. Laurie Mac is just trying her best to make everyone happy. The store has been open for less than a half-hour and is crawling with gorgeous Krispy Kreme public relations people. It's 5:55 a.m. and sheer chaos is ensuing.

It's 6 a.m. BLLLLLAAAAAAAANG!!!!!!!!!!

The K-HITS news theme blasts out over the air, and our live remote has begun. Before we know it our first live shot with anchors Richelle Carey and Marc Cox on KMOV is up. A single camera zeroes in on the four of us, sitting face-to-face at our makeshift broadcast table. I slide in a tiny earpiece underneath one side of my headphones and run the wire around my back and into my pocket, where it plugs into a receiver the size of an iPod. This will allow me to hear the director at the TV station as well as the voices of the anchors.

"Richelle. You're looking a little gaunt! You need to eat some doughnuts!" I explain. The curvaceous Carey squeals with laughter in the manner of someone who hasn't been referred to as "skinny" in a very long time. "There's nothing 'crispy' about Krispy Kreme! We need Allman to launch an immediate investigation!" I tell them. The camera swings over to Laurie and Jennifer who explain why they haven't yet sampled the fare. "I wanted my teeth to be clean for the first shot," Mac says. "Normally I treat my body like a temple," U-Man goes on. "But today I'm gonna treat it like a strip joint on the East Side!"

Cox and Carey lose it.

It'll be another hour-and-a-half until the next TV shot. As we refocus our attention back to the radio side I discover we're not going to be able to walk all over the area of Forsyth and Central and harass people on their way to work as we'd planned. The wireless microphones are operating fine but the "backfeed" system that allows us to hear one another in our headsets isn't getting out more than 20 feet. This is going to have a profound effect on the rest of the broadcast. I'd probably be pissed if it didn't smell so darned good in the place.

It's time for the news but U-Man has slipped away from the table, and we have no idea where he went. BLLLLAAAAAAAAANG!!!!!!!! The news theme hits the air and Laurie, Jen, and I just look at one another. Suddenly we realize we're hearing the faint sound of running water.

"John?" I say into the microphone.

What follows is John's voice, all right. But it's enhanced by a deep echo. By way of his wireless microphone U-Man's voice...and bodily function...are being broadcast over the air, live from a doughnut shop bathroom in Clayton. I think our audience may end up remembering this show.

During the next commercial break, Carl "The Intern" tells me over the two-way that he thinks he has the solution to the problem of the missing *Game Show Network* CD with the *$20,000 Pyramid* theme I need in a few minutes. "You *found* it?!" I ask. "Not exactly," he responds. It's too late for any more discussion about it. KMOV has moved up its "hit time," which means we're on in a few seconds. "Just play whatever you have when I cue you to start the game," I tell him.

The camera zooms in on me. In my fist is a wad of index cards containing the questions for the contest. I have wires hanging off one side of me for TV audio. On my other side dangle all the wires for radio. I figure I must look like the Unabomber. Laurie has pulled two somewhat bewildered people in off the street as contestants. I pair the man with John and the woman with Jen. Back at Channel 4, Richelle and Marc stare at their monitor with a look of complete trepidation.

"It's time to play The 20,000 DOUGHNUT Pyramid!!!!!!" I yell toward the camera. The next sound I hear is the familiar *$20,000 Pyramid* theme music...which Carl and behind-the-scenes programming whiz kid, Ray Collier, are *whistling* in unison into their microphones back at the station.

I love these guys. Just when they sense I'm about to have a total meltdown they totally crack me up with something as bent as this. The game and the live shot come off like a charm.

The show breaks up, as usual, just after 9 a.m. After drawing the winning name for a box of doughnuts every week for a year I'm back to the station by 10:15, where I'm anxious to hear the early reviews on today's show. Everyone is still laughing about John's bathroom segment. I'm even more anxious about the fact the numbers for the all-important spring ratings period are due at 10:30. In just a few minutes lots of people, mostly from sales and programming, will be huddled around the two printers in the building that will spit out the results of the period from mid-April to mid-June. There are a lot of eyes on this ratings book due to our first-place finish in the winter "book" that was released three months ago. Everyone is anticipating another strong finish since this ratings period included the big Opening Day baseball show in April, not to mention our two-week-long 20th Anniversary celebration in May.

I managed to abscond with two dozen Krispy Kremes as I left the broadcast. It's a particularly effective way of staying in the good graces of my pals at the station. The first box gets hand-delivered to the girls upstairs in the sales department at Emmis Broadcasting's newest station, called "Red." Bea is one of my best friends in the building. She's smart, pretty, funnier than she thinks, and one of the nicest, most well-grounded women I know. After four hours every day of acting like a goof and talking on the air with listeners who are often goofier, ten minutes chatting with Bea about her new baby and the other things in her delightfully normal life usually smack me back into reality. It so happens that both my daughters are out of town with their mother for two weeks. I miss them terribly, but I feel a little better after talking with Bea.

I'm back downstairs in my office and watching the clock as I get to work answering e-mail. 10:30 passes. 10:35. 10:40. Finally I head down to the program director's office. One look at his face tells the story. The syndicated *Bob & Tom* radio show that airs on KSHE has edged us out of first place by five-tenths of a point. The margin is so small it's within the bounds of statistical error. He, of course, is elated since he's got the number one, two, and three top morning shows in St. Louis. The "look" on Rick's face is there because he knew how disappointed I'd be to have gotten nudged out of the top spot. He understands things like pride and passion.

I'm back at my desk flipping through the pages of the ratings report. Sara, my knockout account executive friend who sells for KSHE, stops in my doorway and asks, "How'd you guys do?" As I begin with the details a slight grin creeps into her expression. When that turns into a full smile it hits me. She's already seen the results. Three months ago when our show reached number one I teased the crap out of her. She's been waiting that long to get me back. This place is full of smart-asses.

The day isn't going to get any better. It's off to the podiatrist where I'm about to get another cortisone shot straight into my heel. Doctor "Kurt" has been one of my best conservative friends for years and is a huge fan of the show. Today he can't contain himself over how much he's become enamored with Laurie Mac, a staunch, unapologetic liberal. This just cracks me up. I stop laughing when the doc speculates my foot problem may be contributing to my chronic back problem, for which I'm planning to have surgery soon.

Because of the heel problem I have to miss tonight's game in the softball league I've been playing in for four years. I'm the shortstop on a team consisting of men and women, all of whom are at least 10 to 20 years my junior. The trips to the bar afterward are great fun, but I may be the only one on the team who enjoys playing the games more.

My friend Tom calls. He's an old neighbor who operates a commercial plant service that, among other things, decorates the dressing rooms and backstage areas at venues like UMB Pavilion and the Savvis Center. If Elton John's contract rider specifies two four-foot-high ficus plants, Tom's the guy they call. Someone at Savvis has dropped him four primo tickets for Thursday night's Van Halen concert, and he offers them to me for giveaway on the show. Standing in his kitchen we write almost half the questions I'll use in the "Last Man Standing...Famous Brothers" contest that will determine the winner.

Tuesday's show zips by, and I'm back in the office preparing for my third remote broadcast in five days scheduled for tomorrow from Bellerive Country Club. Word comes down that the setup in the media tent won't accommodate all four of us and that U-Man and I will have to leave the girls behind to participate in the show from the studio. Why the hell are we finding out about this *now*? I threaten to pull the plug on the entire broadcast, but that suggestion is overruled. I can tell this is going to be a long day. All of the audio clips I've lifted from *Tin Cup, Caddyshack,* and other movies, plus TV shows have to be edited, mixed with music and dubbed into the computer. Laurie is handling questions from our engineers while going over a long checklist of notes involving the coordination of tomorrow's show. It's about this time that one of our account executives walks in asking for a complete promotional plan involving a potential giveaway of some trips to the Caribbean in the fall. She says she needs it in an hour.

After chopping her into small pieces and burying them behind the building, Laurie and I continue our work.

It's another short night of sleep. Like Monday I have to set the alarm to go off a full hour earlier than usual. After driving downtown to take care of last-minute details, I turn around and head out to West County to the immaculately maintained Bellerive Country Club. It's the kind of place I'd never be allowed within 10 miles of if it wasn't for this job. To call it the media "tent" doesn't accurately characterize the overall magnitude of the facility. Row after row of cubicles with dozens upon dozens of computers armed with plasma TVs and electronics make the place look more like a Circuit City than a country club. Outside, it's a spectacular, chamber-of-commerce summer morning. Inside, the air conditioning is blowing full-tilt. It must be 55 degrees. U-Man is stoked. These are his people. He just can't get enough of anything having to do with golf.

We're told St. Louis' own Hale Irwin may be coming by, but it's rumors of Arnold Palmer's arrival on the grounds that have John nearing his target heart rate. We hand him a wireless microphone (they're working as designed today) and send him outside, up a hill, and around a bend to the tee boxes to have a look around. As soon as I'm sure he's all the way there I tell him Palmer has just walked into the tent. The next thing we hear resembles the sound of a dropped phone combined with the bongo-like sound effect Hanna-Barbera uses when Scooby Doo lays rubber running away from a ghost. Sparks breaks into her best "mall chick" impression to simulate what an encounter between John and Arnie might sound like.

"Oh my God, you're so cute! I totally love you! Can I have my picture taken with you?! I think you're like the cutest guy I've ever seen in my whole, entire life! My girlfriends and I like talk about you all the time! You're my favorite!!"

It takes a moment, but now U-Man is laughing, too.

The cameraman for the Midwest Sports Report arrives to shoot our weekly piece for FOX Sports Net. Because of the last-minute switch in our show's configuration that has Laurie and Jen stuck back at the station, we'll have to make some changes. We'll feed our audio from Bellerive along with the girls' audio at Union Station along with the phone calls we take during the segment *all* through a Walkman laying in the wet grass and into the camera's audio inputs while the camera shoots the video of me and John just outside the media tent. This system has never been tested. We have no idea if it will even work.

When the show is over each of us goes in our own separate direction. Later that night following the Cardinals game I watch for our TV piece. It never runs. Maybe the system failed. Maybe the piece just sucked. I never bothered to ask. This unusually taxing, six-day period is over. We had some good shows and some big laughs, but it's pretty obvious we bit off a lot more than we could chew.

Tomorrow things go back to *normal*. Whatever that means.

20 YEARS OF J.G.

Chapter 14

Photos

In 1983, I was hired by Director Barry Levinson to entertain the extras during long breaks between crowd scenes of *The Natural*. When nobody was looking, I had this photo taken as I sat in Robert Redford's chair.

The entire KSHE staff posed for this Colonel Day's full page ad in 1986. (Back: Don "D.J." Johnson, Joe Mason, J.C., Al Hofer, Cheryl Wiggins, Randy Raley. Front: Mary Tripodi, John Ulett.)

Marcia Brady herself, actress Maureen McCormick, graced our studios at The River in 1995.

St. Patrick's Day 1996 as Steve "The Sportsmonster" Schlanger, Jamie Allman, Karen Kelly, J.C. and Lance Hildebrand motor down Market Street.

Actor Michael J. Fox did our show in 1992 to promote his movie *Doc Hollywood*. The interview was followed by gurney races in the KSD parking lot.

One of the most appealing women I've ever met in the music business was singer/songwriter Melissa Etheridge, who played in our studio at The River in 1995.

When rival KWK tried to crash the KSHE "Kite Fly" at Forest Park in 1985, I smashed into their display with a barrel roll and snapped every kite in half while stupified interns from their station looked on.

Contestants had the opportunity to score prizes by shooting a puck into my mouth during the St. Louis Blues skills competition in the mid-1990s.

Playboy centerfold and St. Louis native Ruth Guerri was a regular on our show at KSHE in the mid-1980s.

Jay Leno frequented my Saturday morning show in the first few months I was on the air at KSHE in 1984.

Believe me, people pay attention when you announce you'll be interviewing *Wheel of Fortune's* Vanna White on a mattress!

Ann and Nancy Wilson of Heart with J.C. at WLUP/Chicago in 1977.

J.C. and the "Red Rocker," Sammy Hagar, backstage at the Arena in 1984.

J.C. interviews actor Tom Selleck following a workout with the Cardinals in the mid-1990s.

One day before the infamous raid on Arnie Warren's KMOX show on the President riverboat at the V.P. Fair, KSHE's Morning Zoo yuks it up with *Playboy* centerfold Maren Jensen, *Airplane's* Robert Hays and Kent McCord of Adam 12.

The worst publicity photo in history! J.C. and "The U-Man" hit the St. Louis airwaves in May of 1984.

Our 1986 publicity photo featuring J.C., Don "D.J." Johnson, John "The U-Man" Ulett and Johnny "Loverboy" Amoroso. Johnny had been an umpire at Johnny Mac's sports complex in Valley Park and later became a regular on the KSHE Morning Zoo.

J.C. at age 13 with his new guitar, velour sweater and genuine "dickey."

KSHE signs on at Union Station in the fall of 1986 with "Layla." (L-R: J.C., Chief Engineer John Oelke, Al Hofer and Program Director Rick Balis. Gary Bennett and General Manager John Beck obscured.)

On the couch backstage at the Westport Playhouse with the Bangles in 1986.

In New York, J.C. visits David Letterman in the mid-1990s at The Ed Sullivan Theatre.

Don Elston's 1959 Chicago Cubs baseball card. Nobody in my neighborhood believed me when I told them he was my uncle.

J.C. on Halloween, circa 1960. Boo!

J.C. and John Ulett during a recent trip to San Francisco.

Jen Sparks, J.C., U-Man and Laurie Mac.

Chapter 15

"Well, they've got a list of all those things of which they don't approve."
"Redneck Friend"
Jackson Browne

Lists and More Lists.

David Letterman figured it out a long time ago. America just loves "Top Ten" lists. Unfortunately, some issues can't be adequately summarized in a list of only ten. Either that or I'm just a sloppy editor because some of the following categories run longer than that.

When you've been talking four hours a day for 20 years, you're bound to get some things right and some things wrong. I've just plain guessed on occasion and been lucky. I've also guessed and prayed nobody remembered what I said. Make enough wrong guesses early in your career in an inexperienced attempt at developing "cutting edge" status and you learn your lesson quickly. Wild guesses get replaced by educated guesses and, more often than not, instinct.

We'll call this the "list" chapter. I've very unscientifically chosen some categories I think are relevant and listed some stuff in no particular order. Here goes.

Top Fifteen Recent, Obscure or Semi-Obscure Movies You've Just Gotta See

One of my pet peeves is seeing people walk into the video store and go directly to the "New Release" wall and mumble about there not being anything good to rent. The shelves are loaded with great films you may have missed when they were in theaters. There are a dozen reasons why a movie may have failed to generate huge box office totals and, of course, it doesn't necessarily follow that great ticket sales equals a great movie. With that in mind, here are some not-so-famous films to look for the next time you're wandering around your neighborhood Blockbuster with a blank look on your face.

1) Office Space

More of an anthem than a movie for anyone who's ever been in a dead-end job or had a passive-aggressive boss. There are scenes in this movie that are so funny you might actually just stare at the screen with your mouth open instead of laughing out loud. Every single supporting player in the film has at least one scene-stealing moment. Jennifer Aniston displays some real comedic brilliance. I have watched this movie more than 50 times. I kid you not.

2) Next Stop Wonderland

Anyone who's ever chosen or been desperate enough to choose a non-traditional dating route will see a lot in this film they recognize. This was a breakthrough role for actress Hope Davis and a chance to see some early work by the usually amazing Philip Seymour Hoffman, the terrific Holland Taylor, and an amusing cameo by comedian Robert Klein, not to mention an amusing subplot about a kidnapped fish. A very smart, very funny, and very romantic movie.

3) The Big Picture

Director Christopher Guest had big hits with films like *Waiting for Guffman* and *Best in Show*, but for some odd reason this highly stylized movie seemed to slip through the cracks. Kevin Bacon stars as a film school prodigy who hits the big time fast, then crashes even faster. It's a lacerating depiction of just how Hollywood operates while providing big laughs, particularly via Martin Short, as well as some moments of genuine poignancy.

4) The King of Comedy

Most people's brains simply shut down over the bizarre notion that a movie starring both Robert DeNiro *and* Jerry Lewis — even if it was directed by Martin Scorsese — could be any good. DeNiro's Rupert Pupkin hatches a plan to kidnap a Johnny Carson-like late night television host in hopes of getting a crack at his national debut as a stand-up comedian. Jerry Lewis as you've never seen him before. A very, very dark comedy.

5) Thirteen Days

Something about the fact this country came to within fifteen minutes of nuclear annihilation has always fascinated me. This is a gripping depiction of the 1962 Cuban Missile Crisis with Bruce Greenwood giving the performance of a lifetime as John F. Kennedy. The film got knocked because Kevin Costner, who plays JFK's chief political advisor, was experiencing a sort of career free-fall at the time it was released. But this entire cast crackles via a brilliant screenplay that genuinely captures the potential world-altering intensity of those historic events without bogging the story down with melodrama. The fact that these events actually occurred makes the presentation that much more powerful.

6) Last Night

So just what *would* it be like if the end of the world was coming and everyone knew the precise moment it would occur? Though it made quite a few "Top Ten of 1999" lists, this Canadian import, sometimes funny, sometimes dark, always significant, went largely unnoticed. There have been many movies that deliver a doomsday theme, but I suspect this is what it would really be like.

7) The Man in the Moon

Reese Witherspoon was just a kid when she made this rural south, coming-of-age film set in the late '50s, but you could see "star" written all over her even then. If you have the patience and appetite for a story that moves at its own pace, sometimes as slow as a lazy, Louisiana creek, you'll be rewarded with a terrific, albeit heartbreaking, family story. There are great supporting roles from Sam Waterston and Tess Harper, plus that groundbreaking performance by Reese Witherspoon. (Not to be confused with *The Man **On** the Moon*, the Jim Carrey flick about Andy Kaufman.)

8) Barcelona

A young, uptight American businessman managing his company's foreign sales office has his world turned upside down in early 1980s post-disco-era Spain when his free-spirited cousin (the same one that accidentally sank his canoe at the family summer home when they were 10) moves in "temporarily." The cousin's U.S. military position sparks troubling and, at the same time, amusing confrontations with the locals. While the movie is, above all, a love story, at the very moment you let your guard down, a plot turn smacks you halfway across the room. I love every single frame of this masterfully assembled movie.

9) Picture Perfect

I'm not sure I've ever seen an entire episode of *Friends*, but for some reason I've found Jennifer Aniston's movie work just terrific. One of her earliest was in 1997 when she starred opposite Jay Mohr as a high-powered ad executive who falls for a wedding videographer. Throw in Kevin Bacon as the ex, Olympia Dukakis as her mom, and the great Kevin Dunn as her boss, and you'll find that director Glen Gordon Caron (of the *Moonlighting* television series) has everything he needs to pull off a top-notch romantic comedy. The speech Mohr delivers to a table of condescending partygoers about why he does what he does for a living, not to mention their stunned reaction, is a real show stopper. Disappointing ending, however, to an otherwise very clever film.

10) Bowfinger

It's hard to imagine this Steve Martin/Eddie Murphy comedy flopped, but that may have been the result of a poor title. Martin is a down-on-his-luck producer/director who figures out a way to have Murphy, one of the biggest names in Hollywood, star in a movie without *knowing* it. Another character is introduced who just happens to be a dead ringer for Murphy's "Kit Ramsey." Throw in a diabolically manipulative starlet played by Heather Graham and some hilarious scenes involving a dog in a parking garage, and you have one of the funniest screwball comedies in years.

11) Return to Me

Presumably the first organ-donor romantic comedy in movie history, Minnie Driver and David Duchovny star as a couple brought together via the strangest of circumstances. Cynics will call it corny, but Bonnie Hunt, who wrote and directed the movie, has a real feel for making us care about these characters. Carroll O'Connor is brilliant in his final movie role and the city of Chicago is lovingly portrayed by hometowner Hunt.

12) The Matchmaker

Say the name Janeane Garofalo and a lot of people head in the opposite direction. But the usually grungy actress cleans up well in this film about a political operative from Boston who's sent to a rural Irish town to try and find a genealogical link to the Kennedy family in an attempt at salvaging the campaign of a Massachusetts senator. What she doesn't know is that she has landed smack in the middle of an old-fashioned matchmaking festival which everyone in the town believes she's done intentionally. Denis Leary co-stars, but it's the stable of eccentric locals that make the movie required viewing around St. Patrick's Day. Oh, and don't forget the Kleenex.

13) The Compleat Beatles

Required viewing for any true fan of the "Fab Four," this documentary traces every significant step in the transformation of four kids from Liverpool into the world's most-famous and important band.

14) Chilly Scenes of Winter

A civil service worker obsesses about how he let the love of his life get away. How many times have you heard that one, right? Well, when it's John Heard and Mary Beth Hurt working off of one of the quirkiest screenplays I've ever seen, this film turns an ordinary love story into a charming-but-neurotic, affectionate-yet-painful, pathetic-but-hilarious depiction of how desperate one man can become over the loss of a woman. The always terrific Peter Riegert plays Heard's womanizing roommate, and the film's director brilliantly uses the bleak Utah winter as yet another desperate character in the story. This obscure movie enjoys a tremendous cult following for good reason.

15) 29th Street

Based on the true story of the first man to win the New York state lottery, this is a funny, warm, and reaffirming film that proves winning a cool six million bucks may actually cause more trouble than it does good. Danny Aiello and Anthony LaPaglia will have you believing they really are father and son. This is a great movie to see during the Christmas season, and I'll pay it the nicest compliment I can. The film has heart.

Top Ten Favorite Celebrity Interviews

We've always been very selective about guests we book on the show, but it's still always a crap shoot. A great guest who's in a bad mood can sink the interview before I ask the first question. Similarly, someone cheerful and enthusiastic can still be a crashing bore. Big stars like Bill Murray or Harrison Ford I'd had high hopes for often produced disappointing results. So, discounting Madonna, the inspiration for my first book, here are ten of the interviews that, for a wide variety of reasons and circumstances, stand out in my memory.

1) Tommy Chong (2003) — We got him only months before he was to serve a one-year sentence on a bizarre, interstate drug paraphernalia charge. Watching this '70s counter-culture icon resigned to the fact that the government had finally figured out a way to get him was a sobering and yet oddly stimulating half-hour.

2) David Letterman (1997) — I was invited to fly to New York for an interview that was supposed to be only seven minutes. Almost a half hour later we were still laughing it up about everything from the lowest point in his career (his having to learn to *dance* for a Mary Tyler Moore variety show he was briefly a part of) to his family ties in Missouri. Dave has been very good to me over the years, sometimes even sending handwritten "thank you" notes following our many conversations. We've laughed about how he appeared to take my head off during a live shot from Lambert Airport about 15 years ago.

3) Gene Siskel (1998) — If you like anything about the way I review movies you have this guy to thank because I learned practically everything I know from watching him and talking with him over the years. Our last interview took place a little less than a year before his untimely death. I made him laugh really hard twice near the end of that conversation. It's how I'll always remember him.

4) Cast of *When Harry Met Sally* (1989) — The movie studio flew me to Vancouver, British Columbia, to see *Lethal Weapon II* and interview Mel Gibson. About a week before the trip a representative called to ask if I'd be interested in staying over an extra night to see a new Rob Reiner film. After seeing the comedy it became clear that the studio had *no idea* what they had. Billy Crystal, Meg Ryan, Reiner and others associated with the movie were gracious but skeptical over all of our collective enthusiasm for what's become one of America's favorite romantic comedies.

5) Moscow DJ (1990) — Sitting in a basement club of a popular tourist hotel we came across a local disc jockey who spoke very good English and was both fascinated with American radio and fascinating to talk with. Frankly, almost everyone we spoke to on the trip was incredibly interesting as it struck us how different these people were from what we'd been taught in school and by our own government.

6) Brian Gibson (1990) — One of the technicians at the Abbey Road Studios in London, this was one of the few guys still around from the old days and who, in fact, engineered the demo for George Harrison's classic,

While My Guitar Gently Weeps. So many of us have tried to imagine what it was like being around the Beatles during their most creative moments in the recording studio. This guy was there for it.

7) Eric Clapton (1989) — I was lucky enough to have an interview scheduled at almost the precise moment that rumors began to surface suggesting there might be a Beatles reunion and that Clapton would serve as John Lennon's replacement. To hear the degree of disdain with which he shot down the idea was a thing of beauty.

8) Phil Alden Robinson (1991) — Normally I interview stars and moviemakers at the time of the release of a film. In this case, I spoke with the director of *Field of Dreams* in the aftermath of the movie's incredible run. What a treat it was to kick around behind-the-scenes stories about the making of the film, including the fact the field was actually painted because the drought that hit the midwest during the summer the movie was in production made it impossible to keep the surface green. This is one of the most gracious, genuinely nice people I've ever met in Hollywood.

9) Melissa Etheridge (1995) — Simply put, one of the most charming, talented, sexy, smart, professional, and genuine women I've ever met. It's the only time in my life that I wished I'd been a gay woman.

10) Steve Allen (1990) — What do you say to one of the great show business icons ever who also happens to be your idol? Whatever it was he must have liked it because I received an autographed copy of his latest book a few days later. I got the distinct impression he had done a lot of interviews that day with people who didn't know much about him. As we covered everything from the old *Tonight Show* to a gangster scene in *My Favorite Year* loosely based on a chapter in his career, he just beamed as he recounted old war stories from television's golden age. This was one of the greatest 20 minutes of my career.

Top Ten Missed Opportunities

Regardless of how well you prepare and how hard you work, failure is an inevitability. But people who know me well understand I'm not bugged as much by failure as I am by missed opportunities. On more than a few occasions I've wanted to bang my head on the edge of a table for being so shortsighted I missed a chance at putting some points on the board.

Here's a few examples that illustrate how bad timing can adversely affect you, or just how dumb one person can be.

1) Drew Carey — After his sitcom with comedian John Caponera, *The Good Life,* was canceled by CBS, and following one or two highly publicized and "unflattering" incidents involving strip joints, I thought his career was all but over. He came into our studio at The River one morning circa 1995 where I proceeded to immediately piss him off with what I thought was a fairly innocuous comment about his hometown of Cleveland, about which he's extremely touchy. The interview was so bad I didn't even save the tape. It wasn't long before he had two new shows that became mega-hits.

2) Kelsey Grammer — In 1988, fresh out of rehab and on the heels of an ugly incident allegedly involving an underage girl, he came in as part of the NHL All-Star Game celebrity game and banquet. He seemed so dazed and bewildered I never even took my recorder out of the bag. Within a few years he was hauling in $1.6 million per episode for *Frasier*.

3) Omaha Weather Job — I'd become great pals with the number one meteorologist in town in the early '80s and made it clear I was serious about breaking into TV weather. Lo and behold, the weekend job opened up, I nailed the audition and was set to hit the air in a few weeks. However, "Dr. Dave," as he was known, got grabbed by the ABC affiliate in Chicago a few days later, the station shuffled some of its personnel around in an attempt at consolidation, and my weekend weather job was eliminated before I ever got to go on the air, thus thwarting "Twister Boy's" big break.

4) Sheryl Crow — For a time in the mid-'90s as we'd be finishing up our show on The River we'd see her, all by herself, tuning her guitar and setting up to play live in the studio during the station's midday show. She never spoke to any of us, so we got the impression she thought we were jerks or something. Because of that experience, I developed a real dislike for her...until I saw her play live at the Pageant for the Mel Carnahan tribute concert in the fall of 2000. I became a believer that night. Now she's one of my absolute favorite singer-songwriters. It's just so odd, though, to think that we were in the same room on several occasions and never spoke.

5) The Rams Super Bowl Year — After being unceremoniously dumped from the KLOU lineup in November of 1998, it would be almost 16 months until I would return to the station. Smack dab in the middle of it all, though, was the Rams' championship season which, as the flagship station for the Rams Radio Network, I would have been in the thick of. As it turned out, Smash did a fine job broadcasting live from Super Bowl week in Atlanta, but I've always felt very detached from that whole experience.

6) Bob Gibson (2003) — At Spring training of 2003 in Jupiter, U-Man and I became involved in a lengthy conversation with the Hall-of-Famer outside the Cardinals clubhouse that he asked us not to record. We figured he was under orders from his attorneys not to do any interviews pending the outcome of an alleged road rage incident in his hometown of Omaha a few months earlier. It was a shame because, for over an hour, he was in an extraordinarily candid mood, covering everything from baseball to civil rights. Had we the opportunity to roll tape it would have ranked among the top two or three interviews I've ever presented on air.

7) Planes, Trains & Automobiles — During one of my many highly publicized "separations" from KSHE in the late '80s, the production crew from the classic film, *Planes, Trains and Automobiles* needed a local on-air talent to record a voice track that would be used for a scene in the film in which John Candy and Steve Martin were listening to the radio on their drive from St. Louis to Chicago. Nobody seemed to know how to reach me, so the gig went to KSHE's Al Hofer who, by the way, did a much better job than I would have.

8) Siskel & Ebert "At the Movies" — I conducted over a dozen interviews, both via satellite and in-person, with Gene Siskel and Roger Ebert throughout the '80s and '90s. I'd frequently get a phone call afterward from their producers who would simply rave about how well the segments had gone and ask me to stay in touch. KMOV cut its budget and the entertainment position — along with my job — was eliminated in December of 1998. When Gene died in January of 1999, those same producers began recruiting movie reviewers from all over the country to do on-air auditions with Roger. In the summer of 1999 I learned they had been looking for me before eventually completing the process and settling on Richard Roeper. I'm certainly not foolish enough to believe I would have had a serious chance at the gig, but it would have been fun to audition.

9) Bruce Springsteen — On the final Saturday of the regular season in September of 1998, Mark McGwire hit home runs number 67 and 68, and the Busch Stadium press box was overflowing with dignitaries, VIP's, and an occasional celebrity. At one point I looked over and there, tucked away in a corner was "The Boss" and his young son. I quickly fumbled for my recorder and approached him for an interview, which resulted in about the most ingratiating shutdown I've ever experienced. He clearly wanted to keep it as private an experience between father and son as possible. Several years later Springsteen would tell Bob Costas that, after that game, he and his son made it halfway to Lambert Airport before they turned around, checked back into their hotel and returned the next day to see Big Mac hit numbers 69 and 70.

10) Helen Slater — The knockout actress made an in-studio appearance at KSHE in 1984 to promote her movie, *Supergirl*, and we just plain hit it off. She asked me to lunch, and I obliged. Two weeks later on *The Tonight Show*, when asked about the multi-city tour to promote the film, she did everything but come right out and say my name. Don't ask me what I was thinking, but I never followed up on it. She went on to star in *Ruthless People, City Slickers,* as well as many other movies and television shows. (El stupido!!)

Top Ten Things I Nailed Early On

1) The Iraq War — There's no way to sugarcoat it. Things got ugly around the station when we, as a group, expressed our disapproval of the Bush administration's decision to invade Iraq. We found ourselves on the receiving end of a wave of angry, accusatory, dismissive, and hostile comments, calls and e-mail, some from inside the station itself. Now, less than two years later, polls show an increasing majority of Americans believe the consequences of this military action were "not worth it."

2) David Frost — When the Mike Danton "murder-for-hire" story splashed, certain members of the media virtually turned their stations over to the controversial Canadian sports agent who insisted, despite official police and FBI accounts and documentation, that he was not the intended target. Why, then, did KMOX take such delight in boasting their novice field reporter, Andy Strickland, had special access to Frost when he (Frost) would prove to be a pathological liar? From nearly day one I told you Frost shouldn't have been viewed as a credible source and that his version of the story would bust.

3) St. Louis 2004 — Heralded in some circles as the biggest thing to hit St. Louis since the invention of toasted ravioli, we were subjected to *seven years* of media hype churned out by out-of-work or underemployed PR types. Their job was to convince all of us that the extravaganza would amount to more than a Ferris wheel, long lines for overpriced food on the Eads Bridge, fireworks and some "B-list" music acts along the riverfront. They didn't and it wasn't.

4) Natalie Portman — Long before she appeared in the *Star Wars* films I saw her in an obscure Timothy Hutton movie called *Beautiful Girls* and started telling everyone who would listen that this kid could turn out to be the next Meryl Streep. I still think so. She's been sensational in everything I ever saw her in. And now she's growing up...so look out.

5) "Field of Dreams" — I saw a sneak preview of this movie with a full audience on a Saturday night in Chesterfield in 1989. Though people walked out of the place in dead silence when the film ended, the whole thing didn't hit me until about an hour later. I raved then and I'm still raving. The 15th anniversary DVD came out in early 2004 and is loaded with goodies.

6) Steve Hartmann — Best known for his "Everybody Has a Story" segments on *The CBS Evening News*, I tracked this guy down and got him on the air long before even his own network realized what they had. Oprah eventually began building entire shows around him, which led to his latest assignment as essayist for *60 Minutes II*. A very nice guy with a unique storytelling skill. As CBS newsman and former St. Louisan Russ Mitchell once told me: "The guy hits it out of the park every time."

7) Kathleen Madigan — Unlike many of our competitors, we've had a long-standing policy of putting only nationally known comedians on *The Showgram*. I played a hunch and made an exception in 1991 and, since then, this local gal has had several dozen Letterman and Leno appearances to her credit, as well as cable specials and impressive finishes on NBC's *Last Comic Standing*. Very funny and a genuinely nice person.

8) Reese Witherspoon — Though I've been terribly disappointed by her recent series of dubious career decisions (*Legally Blonde, Legally Blond Two,* and probably by the time you're reading this, *Legally Blond Three and Four*), there's no questioning her box-office appeal. But a decade ago I saw her first starring role in the coming-of-age film *The Man in the Moon* and knew she was something special.

9) The Corrs — Okay, okay. I admit I found them by accident in March of 1997 when searching for new St. Patrick's Day music and saw three sensational babes on the jacket of their CD. But the music kept getting better and better, and fans were impressed by the fact that they're such accomplished musicians. Their show at the Westport Playhouse three years ago was one of the best live concerts I've ever seen. These girls are so good-looking I think I'd do the brother!

10) James Lipton — The affable host of Bravo's *Inside the Actor's Studio* launched his program with the simple idea of presenting a non-traditional show about show business which focused solely on the art of acting. We presented him in a live interview well before Will Ferrell began spoofing him on *Saturday Night Live*. When you get past the schmaltz and fawning, he routinely asks very good questions that are a product of impressive preparation. (If and when Bravo begins producing DVDs of the show, make an effort to pick up a copy of the episode with Billy Joel. It's one of the best two hours of television I've seen in a long time.)

Ten St. Louis Celebrities I Wish I Could Say I Am As Nice As

With all of the back-stabbing, selfishness and insincerity we encounter doing this job, how refreshing it is when someone reminds us success and impact in the market doesn't necessarily come at the expense of one's grace.

1) Deanne Lane — The KSDK news anchor and reporter is as genuinely sweet today as she was the day I met her nearly 20 years ago. That's very rare in this business.

2) Senator Tom Eagleton — Who could blame him if he walked around with a chip on his shoulder after the way he was treated during the 1972 presidential campaign? Instead, this political icon and rabid baseball fan should be treated as a regional, if not national, treasure.

3) John Goodman — Most of us around here have become so accustomed to seeing him and hearing about him that we've forgotten just how good a guy he is.

4) David Slay — One of the most successful restaurateurs in St. Louis,

David is skilled, gracious and a terrific host.

5) Bob Ramsey — The play-by-play voice of SLU basketball and, occasionally, your St. Louis Cardinals, Bob is talented in styles and areas of broadcasting he hasn't even had an opportunity to display yet. We're talking about a very funny guy here, too. I tried to get him over to be my partner at *101 The Fox* back in the mid-nineties but the guys who controlled the money wouldn't cough up the measly five grand in additional incentive to make the deal happen. I'm happy to say things worked out for all.

6) Bob Costas — Brilliant, funny, and innovative, plain and simple Bob is the best at what he does. As big a deal as he is, it would be awfully easy for him to walk around letting people kiss his ring. Instead, he's gracious and polite with a genuine sense of community. In a business that's gotten louder, more boisterous and, thus, increasingly banal in recent years, Bob continues to raise the bar with class and grace.

7) Joe Bonwich — People who have the job of food and restaurant writer for a newspaper, as Joe does for the *Post-Dispatch*, tend to get a bit on the snooty side with pretentious reviews that border on uselessness for the average reader. But Joe genuinely cares about you having an enjoyable time when you pick out a new restaurant. Good family man, great guest.

8) Jim Woodcock — As Senior Vice President of marketing and communication for the St. Louis Blues, a lot of Jim's time is still taken up trying to undo the nonsense left over from Mike Keenan's reign of terror and the fine work of the incompetent boobs who run the NHL. The good news is he's pretty good at it. A few years ago he assembled a terrific coffee-table book tracing the history of the Blues that sold three thousand more copies than *my* first book. It's a good thing he's such a nice guy or I'd hate him.

9) Vic Porcelli — Pay attention because you won't see me saying such nice things about a direct competitor very often. Of all my years in St. Louis radio I think I laughed the hardest during our shift changeovers from 9:50 to 10 o'clock each morning at The River when Vic used to compile what became known simply as "The List." He has the unique ability to be fun and innocuous without ending up dull and boring. Good guy. (Stop smoking!!!)

10) Dick Ford — By the time you have a chance to read this the venerable Fox2 anchorman may have already slipped into retirement. What a pleasure to have had a desk next to his for six years at KSDK. The news business falls another notch every time an old school guy like Dick disappears from the landscape.

Top Ten Most-Bogus Guests (Or Near Guests)

Man, was this section easy to write. The only difficulty was in trimming the number down to just ten! Everyone in this group has earned a special place on our crash-and-burn list.

1) Susan Powter — The spiky-haired weight-loss guru whose infomercials ruled cable TV in the mid-'90s showed up looking pissed off and with a lot of miles on her. Why she needed an entourage is a mystery, but they were creepy, too. Powter's mood went even darker when I asked about a published report from a reputable magazine in her hometown that claimed she'd worked as an exotic dancer while several months pregnant.

2) Ron Jeremy — A veteran of over seven hundred adult movies, "The Jackie Mason of Porn," as he was once called, demanded he be picked up in a fully stocked, stretch limo. We responded that we didn't even do that for Dana Carvey! Jeremy's "agent" responded, "Well, ask Dana Carvey if he ever f***** Traci Lords!!"

3) Michael Moore — As noted in my first book, the writer/director of *Roger and Me*, *Bowling for Columbine* and *Fahrenheit 9-11* canceled on us a record six times. Finally, he appeared on the show via satellite in 2001, but we never expected him to show so we didn't bother preparing any questions. The guy certainly knows how to make a movie people will talk about, but he seems not to know the first thing about public relations.

4) Dustin Diamond (aka: "Screech") — In 2003 the former star of *Saved by the Bell* toured the country with a stand-up comedy act. He wasn't funny, he refused to talk about the TV show and was just plain snotty about the whole thing.

5) Maureen McCormick — I didn't sleep for a week leading up to her in-studio appearance with us at The River. I was finally going to get to meet *Marcia freakin' Brady!!!* But she turned out to be a real dud. Still very, very cute but not funny, not interesting, nothing to say, except when it got to a stupid country music album she'd just recorded. Sheesh!!!

6) Jamie Farr — We had lots of questions for Corporal Klinger of M***A*S*H***. Unfortunately we never got to most of them because he went on and on about some Vegas resort and casino he was representing. When he gave out the toll-free number for the fifth time in seven minutes we said "goodbye."

7) Joan Rivers — This one-time pioneer for women in comedy went half nuts on me before I even got a question out she didn't like the sound of. This person suffers from a terrible case of inflated self-importance.

8) Bill O'Reilly — He can dish it out, but he can't take it. When I wouldn't let up on him about his moniker "The No Spin Zone," despite the fact that his network operates as a virtual mouthpiece for the Republican party, O'Reilly began insulting the host of the show. That would be me. We don't have a lot of rules, but there is one. Don't insult the host of the show.

9) Stewart Copeland — During one of our live broadcasts from the Grammys in L.A., the ex-drummer for The Police was pushing his new band, Animal Logic. He sat down, saw the slogan "Classic Rock" on our banner, realized our station wouldn't be able to play music from his new CD and began insulting the host of the show. Repeating! We don't have a lot of rules but there is one: See above.

10) Dennis Miller — *TRAITOR!!!!!*

Top Ten Words St. Louisans Mispronounce

It's been more than 20 years since I arrived in town, and I still have no idea how some of these words ended up with these pronunciations. While I refuse to speak like this myself, I gave up the fight to correct people long ago.

1) Highway Farty (Forty)
2) Zink (Sink)
3) Vandeventner (Vandeventer)
4) I-Talian (Italian)
5) Ellinois (Illinois)
6) Uge (Huge)
7) Warshinton (Washington)
8) Expecially (Especially)
9) Acrosst (Across)

10) JC Cochran (JC Corcoran)

Top Thirty-Five Favorite Films of the Past Thirty-Five Years

People always ask me for recommendations on movies. Admittedly my taste runs a little off the beaten path, but excluding the titles mentioned on the *Top Fifteen Recent, Obscure, or Semi-obscure Movies You've Just Gotta See* list earlier in this chapter, here's some of the more recognizable titles from my group of favorites you should see if you already haven't.

1) Breaking Away
2) Grand Canyon
3) Fargo
4) Airplane
5) Field of Dreams
6) Annie Hall
7) The Candidate
8) Election
9) Glen Garry Glen Ross
10) Pulp Fiction
11) Dave
12) Quiz Show
13) Jaws
14) Swingers
15) Return to Me
16) The Sting
17) Fast Times at Ridgemont High
18) All the President's Men
19) Shakespeare in Love
20) Heaven Can Wait
21) Network
22) Defending Your Life
23) Slingblade
24) Roger and Me
25) It's A Wonderful Life*
26) My Favorite Year

27) Best Friends
28) She's Having a Baby
29) Goodfellas
30) Rocky
31) Philadelphia
32) Tootsie
33) One Flew Over the Cuckoo's Nest
34) The Shawshank Redemption
35) The Godfather

*(Though released in the mid 1940s, director Frank Capra kept the film out of distribution until the mid-'70s, which supports the notion it could qualify for this list. If you disagree, write your own book.)

Top Twenty Favorite Songs

1) I Dreamed Last Night — Bluejays*
2) Mysterious Ways — U2
3) Change — Sheryl Crow
4) Nantucket Sleighride — Mountain
5) French Waltz — Nicolette Larson
6) Won't Get Fooled Again — The Who
7) Let It Grow — Eric Clapton
8) God Only Knows — Beach Boys
9) Life's Been Good — Joe Walsh
10) Taxi — Harry Chapin
11) Golden Slumbers — Beatles
12) Like It Or Not — Genesis
13) A Man I'll Never Be — Boston
14) In the Wee Small Hours of the Morning — Frank Sinatra
15) Tangled Up in Blue — Bob Dylan
16) No Frontiers — The Corrs
17) Long, Long Time — Linda Ronstadt
18) Behind Blue Eyes — The Who
19) In the Shape of a Heart — Jackson Browne
20) We Can Work It Out — Beatles

*(Justin Hayward and John Lodge's 1975 joint effort following the

brief disbandment of *The Moody Blues*.)

Top Ten Nicest National Celebrities

1) Jay Leno
2) Pat Sajak & Vanna White
3) Meg Ryan
4) Dustin Hoffman
5) John Travolta
6) Dolly Parton
7) Drew Barrymore
8) Dana Carvey
9) Mike Myers
10) Super Dave Osborne

Top Fifteen Memorabilia Owned by J.C.

1) A limited-edition 1978 *Darkness On the Edge of Town* Bruce Springsteen picture disc.

2) A handwritten letter from Mick Jagger to Chuck Berry I read onstage as part of my emceeing duties at the filming of *Hail, Hail Rock & Roll* at the Fox Theater in November of 1986.

3) Stan Musial's early 1960s instructional-hitting album personally autographed to me.

4) An autographed, limited-edition color ink drawing of the band by John Entwistle of *The Who*.

5) A limited-edition bronze beaver paperweight from *The Naked Gun* autographed to me by David Zucker, co-writer and co-director.

6) A box of White House M&Ms emblazoned with the presidential seal and signature from the trunk of Bill Clinton's limousine during a 1996 campaign stop.

7) A CD copy of *Who's Next* autographed to me by Roger Daltrey.

8) A copy of *Annie Hall* autographed to me by Woody Allen.

9) My press pass from 8-8-88, the first-ever scheduled night game at Wrigley Field.

10) An *Imagine* ring personally sent to me by Yoko Ono after she was forced to cancel a scheduled interview.

11) A personally autographed Derek Jeter baseball bat.

12) A baseball individually signed by the 1956 Brooklyn Dodgers.

13) A personally autographed tennis racket by Ken Flach actually used in his mens' doubles championship match at Wimbledon.

14) A autographed Brett Hull hockey stick.

15) A copy of the *Fast Times at Ridgemont High* soundtrack autographed by writer Cameron Crowe.

Top Two Celebrities I Would Have Wanted to Interview

1) Johnny Carson

2) Curly Howard

Top Two Regrets in Life

1) Never having tried to make it at Second City

2) Never learning to play the piano

Chapter 16

"What is this power you speak of and the need for things to change? I always thought that everything was fine."
"Dialogue"
Chicago

Mini-Rants.

George W. Bush ran his 2000 campaign under the slogan, "I'm a uniter, not a divider." Now, four years later this country finds itself more angrily divided than at any time since the Vietnam War era.

One of the ongoing kicks I get doing this show is opening e-mail from listeners who write some version of the following: "I couldn't disagree with you more, politically, but I love the show. Keep up the good work."

I'm puzzled by the fact a measurable chunk of the audience doesn't understand that our on-air discussion of politics isn't intended to be taken any more seriously than the monologues of Letterman, Leno, Stewart, and Maher. Because I'm not certain anyone really knows what my politics are and because I've been on the receiving end of so many bizarre calls and e-mails pertaining to this topic, I want to spend a little time on it. I'm not, I repeat, I'm *not* trying to change anyone's mind.

I believe our political system has been broken for quite some time. The problem is money. The second a politician gets elected he or she must begin cutting deals and selling his or her soul in order to maintain the massive fundraising effort that's necessary to get re-elected. It's a system tailor made for corruption. I'd be in favor of designating dollar figures that could not be exceeded by anyone or any group during an election year.

I don't like the term "our leaders." These clowns aren't leading me anywhere.

I don't like boneheads messing with the system. That includes *all* one-sided political talk show hosts. By the way, "talk radio" involves an exchange of disparate thoughts and ideas. Most of today's talk radio is propaganda. Anyone who can't say the word "judges" without prefacing it with "radical" or "environmentalist" and tagging it with "wackos" has a political agenda and isn't trying to prompt an open discussion. And a doctor-shopping, "hillbilly heroin"-slamming, loose-with-the-truth oaf deserves to be shunned, not respected.

I think Michael Moore is a riot. He also does at least one thing in each of his films to ruin it.

I don't understand how conservatives preach endlessly about less government, then try to dictate what may and may not be done in the most private of environs, the bedroom.

Forty percent of Americans surveyed six weeks before the presidential election of 2004 said they believed Saddam Hussein was responsible for the 9-11 attack. I know you can't make people take a test before you allow them to vote, but maybe we should think about it, huh?

Political operatives are gumming up the entire system with issues that prompt visceral responses. Stuff involving the "Pledge of Allegiance," flag-burning amendments, gay marriage, and partial-birth abortion affect less than one percent of the population but are taking up 90 percent of the time. Meanwhile, while we waste our time arguing about it, their bosses are robbing us blind!

"Act Up" and "PETA" people annoy the crap out of me.

The conservatives' efforts at "social engineering" annoy the crap out of me.

The gay community is just like any other community of individuals. They have one whole group running around in underpants and another whole group that's just like you and me.

Why do non-whites get judged by the worst examples in their group while whites get to be judged by the best examples in their group?

Most of "Homeland Security" is a joke. Anyone who wants to can enter the service or construction areas of most airports and drive right out onto a runway. In the meantime, we have this ridiculous "theater" that goes on every day during which passengers are being groped, undressed, and examined to make it appear as though we're really doing something about security. Screeners at LAX actually boasted that they once pulled *Ray Charles* aside for additional scrutiny because his name came up on their random system. That's not something they should be proud to admit to!

Racial profiling is a bum deal. But "social" profiling based on likelihood and probability is a necessary evil. It's not the Swedes who are mad at us.

Too much racial profiling isn't necessary anyway. Find out who the bad guys are and leave everyone else alone.

We're gunking up our entire criminal court and prison system busting people for smoking pot. Don't buy into that nonsense about everyone who's on heroin now having begun with marijuana. Baloney! They all started with the "legal" drug...*beer!!*

Who you get your news from predicates what you will end up believing. Beware of news operations that look almost exactly like the real media but aren't.

As long as they know what they're talking about, celebrities who speak their mind politically should be admired, not criticized. They actually have a lot to lose, and that makes their choice to speak up admirable, to say the least.

The idea of telling residents of a community not to cook out, fill their gas tanks, mow their lawn or travel during the middle of the summer tourism season is the height of absurdity, especially when things like buses and industrial complexes are allowed to pour tons of filth into the air ad nauseum. If you want a "Clean Air Program," start by leaning on the biggest offenders.

Whatya mean you can't proposition your wife in a sex club?

Don't be surprised if I don't look as though I'm in a big hurry to be friends with you if we exist on opposite sides of the political spectrum. In this day and age your politics are who you *are*, and if you're not part of the solution you're part of the problem.

Staging 4th of July hot-dog-eating contests is only making the terrorists from the other side of the world hate us more.

Downtown St. Louis will never experience significant revitalization until the forces that be understand what Cleveland, Milwaukee, Chicago, Baltimore, and virtually every other major city located next to water understands. Build adjacent to the water, stupid! Credit Bernie Miklasz for suggesting Joe Edwards be given the opportunity to do for downtown St. Louis what he's done with University City's "Loop." And develop things that will attract single people and tourists. What's with this bizarre obsession with making every activity in this town "fun for the entire family?"

SUVs aren't bad. SUVs driven by people who don't need them *are*. But the larger problem is that it's a known fact that Detroit has the capacity to mass-produce fuel efficient SUVs, but doesn't.

Hubert Humphrey said, "Everyone has the right to be heard...but not necessarily to be taken seriously." It's one of the wisest things ever uttered by a politician.

...And as long as I'm on a roll, here are some additional thoughts that are more social than political in nature, but still guaranteed to get you into a good argument.

It's bad enough that so much of the Internet is clogged with goofs trying to sell you something you don't want or need. But somebody is going to eventually have to do something about what I call "Internet terrorism" — the act of nameless, faceless cowards who attempt to destroy peoples' reputations by flooding chat rooms, message boards and e-mail with lies and innuendo. I believe this will become a very big story in coming years.

There is more truth in George Carlin's famous "Baseball vs. Football" routine than most people would like to admit. Without question, the morons who have been running baseball for the last decade have done everything in their power to ruin the game, and the overall state of sports in this country has changed so much that even baseball has gotten sucked into the corporate machine. But the feeling I get just walking into a baseball game is so vastly different from the overall football experience that it tells the whole story. I see families, fathers holding their young sons' and daughters' hands, walking to their seats at Busch Stadium. At the Dome, I see huge, grunting, howling oafs stuffed into gaudy outfits ingesting gagging amounts of food and drink...all before 12 noon. Football, with its PSLs, ostentatious luxury boxes and outrageous prices for *everything* has become a festival of excess. Baseball, it seems to me, is still about the game.

Politicians make lousy guests. *Ex*-politicians make terrific guests.

Just because someone is a gifted athlete doesn't necessarily make them interesting or likeable. Apply the same rule to entertainers and movie stars. Musicians, particularly singer/songwriters, tend to be worth talking to.

Brainstorming sessions. Karaoke. Motivational Speakers. Bed and Breakfasts. The new breed of country music. ALL BAD!

First, brainstorming sessions. Only creative people who have demonstrated an aptitude for analyzing a situation and coming up with ways to make it better should be allowed to influence policy, direction, systems and schemes. Don't confuse ideas with *good* ideas. Tossing a handful of gumshoe sales people into a room and expecting innovative new ideas to come of it couldn't be any more ridiculous. "Facilitators" are scam artists trying to make money. This is a racket!

Next, karaoke. This is entertainment from the bowels of hell that was sort of a cute idea for awhile. The Pet Rock, the Rubik's Cube and Pictionary all knew when their run was over and made a graceful but necessary exit from American pop culture. Let me break some bad news to you: not everyone can sing! Not everyone deserves to make sounds into a microphone! It's a *priv-e-lege* that is earned by people born with a gift that they've worked to develop. You wanna sing? Sing in the shower!

Next, bed and breakfasts. I don't eat breakfast. I'm working at that hour, plus breakfast food is all fatty and greasy and runny. Now, it's just a bed. But I fall asleep on the couch or in my recliner watching TV most of the time. Now it's nothing.

Next, motivational speakers. If you want to give your employees a day off let them play golf.

Finally, the new breed of country music is a big lie. It's been over-commercialized, corporatized, and sexualized. Not only is it in no way true to its original roots and form, but it evolved into a modern-day, watered-down version of pop music, complete with overblown production and marketing. Many of rock music's icons are still musically active, still recording, still touring, and still receiving significant airplay. Most of country music's icons have been reduced to guest presenters at the industry's yearly awards show. The camera angles, set design, and overall style of Garth Brooks' videos at his peak of popularity in the mid-'90s strongly resembled the videos of Van Halen and other rock music acts. For the first Shania Twain network TV special, a camera positioned in the orchestra pit in front of the stage shot straight up into her black mini-skirt, which was roughly the length of a belt. Now *that's* country!

Incidentally, one of the country music stations in St. Louis has a new slogan. It reads: "The Bull Rocks." Hey! Country can't "rock." *Rock* "rocks," doofus!

There you have it. That's where I stand on all the important issues of the day. It all looks so logical to me. Can we stop fighting now?

Chapter 16

"I don't pretend to understand women's little quirks.
One thing I can say for sure: Chicks dig jerks."
"Chicks Dig Jerks"
Bill Hicks

The National Jerk Test

One of my earliest broadcast influences was Steve Allen. In fact, he's one of the main reasons I'm in this business.

In my first book I recalled childhood memories of negotiating with my parents to be allowed to watch his network television show in the early 1960s which he'd open each night with a stunt. It might have been anything from wing walking, being spread eagle in the inside of a churning cement mixer, or having himself lowered into a giant tank of dip while wearing a suit of chips. (That bit would be replicated in the 1990's by David Letterman, who also acknowledged Allen's genius.) Later in the decade, I remember Allen's evening syndicated show being one of the funniest things I'd ever seen.

Though Steve Allen became somewhat bitter and disillusioned in his later life, taking out full-page ads in newspapers around the country to object to most of what he saw on the networks' prime-time schedule, there's no questioning his brilliance. Fifty years ago he virtually invented the TV talk show format that's still being used today.

About 20 years ago Allen had a best-selling humor book that contained something called "The National Jerk Test." He surmised a lot of people were walking around acting like jerks who didn't *know* they were jerks. "A bricklayer," he reasoned, "knows he's a bricklayer, and a baseball player knows what he is, too. But a jerk rarely perceives himself as a jerk."

When Steve Allen issued the test over 20 years ago, questions ranged from "Have you ever thrown a roll of toilet paper at a football game?" to

"Have you ever blown your car horn in a tunnel?" Unfortunately, manners and behavior in this country have deteriorated at such an alarming rate in the past two decades that Allen's test has become completely outdated. So, as a public service and as *homage* to one of my early broadcasting heroes, here is the updated "National Jerk Test."

Individually, some of these infractions aren't indicative of jerkdom. Add up a bunch and...well...

Respond to all fifty questions honestly, give yourself one point for every "yes" answer and see where you stand. Good luck...and I already know you're all going to cheat!

The Updated "National Jerk Test"

1) Do you stand up or dance at concerts, thus blocking the view of others who have paid hundreds of dollars to see the show?

2) Do you fail to tip in restaurants even when the service has been good?

3) Do you speak loudly while conducting a conversation while using a hands-free cellular phone in a public place?

4) Do you run onto an elevator before first allowing the other riders the opportunity to get off?

5) Do you talk during movies in theaters?

6) Do you allow your small children to get up from the table at restaurants and run around?

7) Do you refuse to move out of the passing lane on highways, tailgate other drivers, or regularly fail to use your directional signals?

8) Do you chew food with your mouth open?

9) Are you a slob in public?

10) When intoxicated, do you refuse to give your car keys to a friend even after being approached multiple times?

11) Are you passive-aggressive?

12) Do you gossip?

13) Do you smoke in restaurants, on the beach, or at swimming pools?

14) When you're fortunate enough to get baseball tickets behind home plate, do you call friends on your cell phone and wave incessantly at the center field camera?

15) When paying by check at the grocery store, do you wait until after your total has been rung up before you take your checkbook out and begin writing?

16) Do you allow yourself to swell to over a hundred pounds overweight and then expect preferential treatment because of your size?

17) Are you snotty to clerks, waiters, and waitresses?

18) Do you litter?

19) Do you park with your wheels over the lines in public lots?

20) Do you allow your dog to defecate on neighbors' lawns?

21) Do you operate a lawn mower or leaf blower before 9 a.m. on weekends?

22) Do you force friends and co-workers to look at unreasonable amounts of baby pictures and vacation videos and photos?

23) In your view, did that Timothy McVeigh get a raw deal?

24) Do you drive fast in shopping center parking lots?

25) Do you attend church on Sunday, then fail to conduct your life in any way similar to God's teachings?

26) Do you argue that the answer to reducing violent crime is more handguns?

27) When attending pro sports events, do you let out lots of piercing whistles or yell personal messages at the players from long distances even though you're so far away they can't possibly hear you?

28) Do you park yourself on an escalator like a bag of cement requiring everyone behind you to wait until you're off?

29) Have you ever pledged money to a charity or telethon and not paid?

30) Do you spend a lot of time insisting jazz is better than rock?

31) At parties, have you ever "double-dipped" in the dip or salsa bowl?

32) Have you ever struck your children or verbally abused them in public?

33) If you are a minority, do you expect people to get out of your way or make special accommodations for you?

34) If you are not a minority, do you go out of your way to make trouble for people who are?

35) Do you naturally assume people will be entertained by jokes containing racial slurs or stereotypes?

36) Do you think motorcycles should be allowed to have excessively loud, unmuffled engines and that cars should be allowed to have giant, eight-million-watt stereo systems?

37) Are you always late for everything?

38) Do you have antagonistic, blatantly pugnacious political or abortion-related bumper stickers on your car?

39) At professional sporting events, do you nudge kids out of your way to get players' autographs?

40) Do you often "correct" people in social or family situations?

41) Do you argue that good grammar and effective use of language really aren't very important?

42) Do you think that the fact a person doesn't share your opinions automatically makes them an idiot?

43) Do you do most of your hanging around with people whom others consider jerks?

44) Do you think Bill O'Reilly possesses a brilliant interviewing style?

45) In social situations do you always need to be the center of attention?

46) Because you display the American flag on your property, car, truck, or clothing, do you believe you're more patriotic than people who don't?

47) Do you make fun of people or laugh behind their backs when a pet of theirs dies?

48) Do you think the *National Enquirer* and paparazzi have a right to stalk and invade the privacy of celebrities?

49) Do you bring children into areas marked "no children"?

50) Do you cut in lines?

Totals

0 to 6 points:

Good news! You're not a jerk. Even though you may do something jerky on occasion, apparently you apply such good social judgment the rest of the time that few around you notice or remember it. Please breed! And when you do, train your offspring to behave as you do.

7 to 12 points:

Good news! You're not a jerk, either. Bad news. You could be on your way to becoming one. Stop! Reflect. Ask yourself if your patterns of social interaction have been slipping. You might want to ask some friends and family members if they've been discussing whether to continue including you in group activities. More good news: You may have caught this in time. In other words, this test may have saved you!

13 to 18 points:

Congratulations! All that big-butt talk has finally caught up with you. It's not your imagination. People *do* stop talking when you walk into a room. Oh...and they roll their eyes back in their head when you leave, too. The only reason co-workers even talk to you anymore is when they want to know who was on *Mad TV.* That's because they know you're always home on Saturday nights!

19 to 24 points:

How does it feel to be a real jerk? There are trained professionals who could help, but you'd rationalize it all away. It's been years since you gave a rat's ass about anyone other than yourself. Have you noticed people keep walking when you try to talk to them? That's all for now. I don't want to keep you. I'm sure you have to go start a fight or something.

25 points and higher:

Not only are you a jerk, but you actually enjoy it! You suck! Even a month locked in a sensory-deprivation tank with Dr. Phil couldn't save you. Even the kid in the mail room with the b.o. and the lazy eye doesn't want to have anything to do with you. You exhibit the rare combination of being loud *and* stupid. You couldn't even get a dog to play with you if you had a pork chop tied around your waist. Quick! Look up! It's the president flying over to declare you a disaster area.

(*Editor's note:* JC received a score of "4." Good luck figuring out which four.)

Chapter 17

"Why do we never get an answer when we're knocking on the door with a thousand million questions about hate and death and war."
"Question"
The Moody Blues

Coming up in the business I asked a lot of questions of people whom I respected as good interviewers. Larry King told me one of the keys is being selective about whom you choose to interview in the first place. Oprah stressed the importance of asking what you really want to know. (Terrific advice!) Joe Garagiola said preparation was the most important part of the process. I paid lots of attention, made lots of mistakes, and one day I realized I knew what I was doing.

Whether it's a reporter from the *Post-Dispatch* or some high school kid doing a class assignment, people have been asking me a lot of the same questions since I got to St. Louis 20 years ago, and they're rarely the kinds of questions that lead to particularly revealing responses. So, to take care of that problem, here it is. For the first time ever, J.C. Corcoran is interviewed by a guy a lot of people think is one of the best interviewers in town: J.C. Corcoran.

JC's Interview With JC.

INT: First off, let me say you look great.

JC: Thanks. So do you.

INT: Why did you agree to do this interview?

JC: I've heard you're very good. Also, in all the years I've been doing these things, I've never felt a lot of the interviews really scratched the surface of what I'm all about.

INT: Okay, then. Here's your chance. What are you all about?

JC: Well, I think if you listen to the show, and you think you know me, you're probably sadly mistaken. You have to remember that I let the audience know exactly the amount about my life I *want* them to know. I think most people would be pretty surprised to learn how "schizy" my life is. I have this sort of noisy, high-profile job in the morning often followed by more stuff later in the day that's related to the job — like celebrity interviews, movie screenings, and travel to exciting locations to do the show. Now that's what most people probably think my whole life is like. What they don't understand is the rest of the time I'm a single dad, which means I'm usually functioning as a short-order cook, chauffeur, and "referee." And by that I mean trying to get in between a nine- and eleven-year-old before they leave permanent marks on one another. Anyhow, the phrase "pick-up line" used to mean something a lot different to me than it means now. Every afternoon it's about two hundred women in SUVs...and me...in the pick-up line at my daughters' school.

INT: And how are you generally received in situations like that?

JC: Depends. Most people are usually very cordial. There are always some dirty looks anyplace I go in public. I always wonder what it was that made them hate me, and if it was about something I really did or just something they thought I did. Once I found out the friend of a woman I was dating hated me because of something she said I did on the air about 15 years ago. She said I was broadcasting from the top of the Arch and tossing stereos and televisions down to the listeners as part of a game called "Catch It and You Keep It." Only one problem. It wasn't me. It was a bit Smash did at KSHE for April Fools Day.

INT: And this woman has hated you all this time, and it wasn't even you, and it wasn't even *real*?

JC: Exactly.

INT: You've mentioned on the air your daughters go to Catholic school.

JC: That's not a question.

INT: Um.... May I finish?

JC: Sorry.

INT: You've been pretty tough on the Catholic Church over the years and, some might say, on Christianity in general. How do you reconcile that? And might that be part of the reason for those occasional dirty looks?

JC: Actually, I'm very surprised at how weak the link is between the church and a big chunk of the parishioners. I always just assumed all of the mothers and fathers in the parish are a hundred per cent onboard with all of the church's policies. Then you talk to them after they've had a few beers at the school picnic, and you find out otherwise. This is the second year I'll be emceeing a major fundraiser for the school. I take part in, or at least show up for, most of the other events. I like a lot of the people, and I always spend moments with the monsignor. I think guys like that are amazing individuals. Just think about the sacrifices they've made in life in order to do what they do. I'm not a practicing Catholic. I have sort of the stereotypical love-hate relationship with the church, having been beaten early and often in the Chicago archdiocesan school system followed by four years in an all-boys Catholic high school. I don't like the church and the schools mixing conservative politics into what they're teaching, but I also respect their passion for what they believe. The worst thing about the abuse scandal that's rocked the church in recent years is the victims. But the second worst thing is the way the honest, dedicated, hardworking majority of people connected with the church have been dirtied up. I have a friend who, at the peak of the abuse scandal, went to a party with a young priest who was dressed in lay clothes. The priest asked my friend not to tell anybody at the party what he does for a living. Now that's just sad.

INT: So you're saying you're not, as some callers to the show have suggested, "anti-Christian"?

JC: Absolutely not. I just don't buy into most religious dogma, a lot of stuff in the Bible, or even the idea that it makes any sense to put three hundred people in a room each Sunday when everyone's concept of God is different anyhow. I see prayer as the ultimate in egomania. To think the almighty force should be expected to care about your stupid football game...come on! I was amused by the media's characterization of America's "return to religion" after the September 11th attacks. I guess I don't have to tell you the churches returned to their normal attendance figures about six months later. By the way, do you know if you tell a doctor you're hearing voices he'll lock you away for treatment? But if you say that voice is God's...

INT: So, it sounds like what you're really saying is you're extremely irritated by hypocrisy.

JC: Exactly! For example, there's an interesting organization called the Fellowship of Christian Athletes. They have a chapter here in St. Louis and a lot of very fine men like Andy Van Slyke, Todd Worrell, and Ricky Horton do some good community work and keep young sports stars in line and away from a lot of the temptations those guys often fall prey to. By the same token, there's one guy who pitched for the Cardinals in the '80s who's always been part of that organization and who was very proud of his reputation for being, shall we say, most "active" on the road. Now, this guy had a wife and kids and anybody who spent any time at all covering those teams during that period knew all about it. And he wasn't the only one. By the way, you know those end zone shots during NFL games when there's an extra point or field goal attempt? Ever wonder how there always seems to be a *John: 3:16* or "Trust Jesus" sign perfectly positioned between the uprights? That's your Fellowship of Christian Athletes hard at work securing those seats all over the league.

INT: And all of this means what?

JC: It's just silly and a little disingenuous. Isaac Bruce, for example, says he prayed over a cell phone with his sister in the locker room after he pulled a hamstring in a pre-game warm-up and that the praying healed him. What? Doesn't Isaac think the guys in the opposing locker room are praying, too? That was part of that whole "God-has-a-plan-for-the-Rams" deal a few years ago. I love the fact that they only thank God when they win. And now the kid who races onto the field to retrieve the tee after the kick-off blesses himself and points to heaven after he charges back to the sidelines. Like I said. Silly.

INT: What do you do? Collect stories like this or something?

JC: No. There are examples every day, though. When Hurricane Ivan flattened Granada and looked as if it was about to make a direct hit on Jamaica, KSDK meteorologist Mike Roberts told people on the air to pray. Then, when it missed to the south of the island, he said their prayers had been answered. So, what? The people on Granada didn't pray *well* enough? Is that what the message was? The next day he said, "If hurricanes have angels, they were hard at work last night guiding this storm." It's like Laurie Mac said, maybe it's a new gimmick, "Religion and weather together?" Gimme a break!

INT: Okay, then what *do* you believe?

JC: There have been lots of nights in my life when I've wondered how I was going to get out of a serious mess I was in or how I was going to make it to the next morning. Both personally and professionally, I've found myself in some situations not even my closest friends or family will ever know about. And I'm not saying that to be melodramatic. I mean it. But compared to what I see some people having to go through, I'd never try to convince anyone I've had a difficult life. Everything's relative, though. So when I look back and consider how bad some situations *could* have gotten but didn't, I can't help but feel the sensation that someone or some thing has been looking out for me. Now, I've developed a healthy respect for whatever that thing is, but I don't know why I should have to combine the devout sense of conscience that comes along with it with conventional, formalized religious trappings. Too many rules. Too many double standards. Kids are taught about the "holy ghost," but they can't pretend to believe in other ghosts one night a year at Halloween.

INT: You said you went to Catholic school followed by four years of an all-boys Catholic high school. Were you ever an altar boy?

JC: They wouldn't let me.

INT: Did you do something?

JC: What I'm doing now.

INT: You spend a lot of time on the air talking about the conservative right and its connection to things like religion and patriotism. This really bugs you, doesn't it?

JC: Well, no conservative has ever been able to explain how the Bible is all about turning the other cheek, caring for your fellow man and peace, but the conservatives always seem to be first to support war efforts, cut social programs, and grind their heels in on social issues that keep the world from being more peaceful. If you go to a football game at the Dome, during *The Star-Spangled Banner* they project images of fighter planes and military stuff on the Jumbotron. Why isn't our national anthem "America the Beautiful," and why aren't we seeing pictures of the amber waves of grain or black and white kids playing together in a spirit of brotherhood like the song says? Yes. The suggestion is that military overkill equates to some weird form of patriotism and that the whole concept is embraced and promoted by conservatives, bugs the crap out of me.

INT: At the beginning of...

JC: WAIT! I wasn't finished!

INT: Sorry.

JC: For a few years I got hooked on "Christian" radio. There are a couple stations that bill themselves that way here in town. I'm talking "Focus on the Family," "The BOT Radio Network," "The Promise Keepers" convention broadcast. The works! And you know what? There's hardly any "Christian" talk that goes on! It's almost all right-wing politics they're kicking around! I find that amazing, and I think most people would, too, if they knew it was happening, particularly people who might be in a position to ask questions about their tax-exempt status.

INT: So, aren't you happier when there's a conservative in the White House? It sounds like it gives you more material for the show.

JC: At the expense of the country? Yes. But that having been said, anyone doing any form of comedy still thanks the Lord for the eight years Bill Clinton was in office. Did you know the Monica thing almost brought Johnny Carson out of retirement? I'm serious. That should tell you something.

INT: You sound incredibly grouchy on the air some days. Is that real or is that part of your schtick?

JC: Both. I'm like everyone else. Some days I really am pissed about something. Most days I'm probably amplifying something to make it into a bit. We laugh about it as soon as the microphones get turned off.

INT: People think of a guy like Jack Buck who was arguably the most popular broadcaster in St. Louis history, and he was so nice all the time. Has it ever occurred to you that you're doing this all wrong and that the way to become the most successful is to be nice all the time?

JC: First off, we have some out-takes of Jack Buck where he had a mouth like a sailor, so at least some of that was image just like anybody else, but he was always very classy in public. Second, that schtick worked for Jack, but it wouldn't work for most of us, and it probably wouldn't even work for Jack if he were our age and trying to compete in the current environment, especially in the mornings. Besides, look at Mark Klose. Actually that's cruel and unusual punishment. Let me rephrase that. Take Mark Klose, for example. Everyone you talk to thinks of him as the nicest guy on radio, and all of the research backs that up. Well, in the 20 years that I've been here, Klose has actually moved around from station to station more than I have. What does that tell you? This is just a goofy business where things can change overnight. Sometimes you simply have to get out. Sometimes they do it for you.

INT: The rudeness factor in morning radio, particularly, has risen exponentially in the past 20 years, and a lot of people blame guys like you for the effect it's had on society, especially kids. Do you accept any of the blame?

JC: Nope. First of all, television and print are more likely to set trends, especially among kids. Radio is more likely to follow trends. It's a real "monkey see, monkey do" business. Songs and musical styles you hear, and styles of radio you hear almost always exist because they were successful somewhere else. Next, our kind of station doesn't even have any kids listening unless, of course, their parents have it on in which case it's their responsibility, not mine. My kids, for example, aren't allowed to listen to 95 percent of what I do. The show is for adults. This goes back to what I was talking about earlier. Radio is just too attractive a target for anyone who's looking to play the blame game. Besides, I'm old school about this stuff in my personal life. Consider the odd reactions I get when I hold doors open for women. They look at me like it's a trick or something. I'm a "please and thank you" kind of guy, and my daughters have been raised to be that way, also.

INT: You hang up on callers all the time!

JC: People can say whatever they want, within reason, when they call in. You don't get hung up on for disagreeing with the hosts. You get hung up on for being a jerk. Now, there are some callers who get hung up on that understand I'm doing it for effect. Those people get it, though. They understand they're part of the show.

INT: So all this rudeness had to come from somewhere?

JC: I think it all started with those commercials where the lady yells, "Hey, Culligan Man!!!" What the hell kind of way is that to talk to someone?

INT: And not "shock radio"?

JC: Well, as I've said before, I do not now, nor have I ever engaged in, "shock radio." The news media really locked onto that moniker in the mid-'90s and started tossing it around without having any idea what the hell they were talking about. It's the height of irresponsibility to misapply that term. It's like calling a lawyer an "ambulance chaser" or a writer a "hack."

INT: So, then, what is "shock radio"?

JC: It's an industry term that specifically defines a style pretty much created by Howard Stern: strippers, lesbians, derogatory remarks targeting certain groups, a fixation on vulgar language, racially charged remarks, crude humor...

INT: Don't you do that sometimes?

JC: Ah ha! There you have the distinction. *"Sometimes."* There is a huge difference between doing occasional crude humor and allowing it to define you. The overwhelming amount of time on our show we're talking about what's going on in the world and in the city. We're laughing and talking with callers, and there's a fairly friendly spirit to things. We'll make a joke about a minority, but there's never a *pattern* of ridicule like there is in the one-dimensional world of shock radio. Besides, if you sat there with a scorecard, you'd find we spend the largest percentage of the time ripping on each other!

INT: Does the station get lots of complaints about your show now?

JC: Yup. This is going to sound odd, but that's how I knew the show had hit big. Only when you have an enormous audience do the complaint calls start rolling in. The bigger the audience, the greater the likelihood you're reaching new listeners not familiar with you and, thus, much more likely not to *get it.*

INT: Is there a recurring topic in those complaints?

JC: Right now it's politics 'cuz we're in an election year. Before that it was the war. I'll tell you something interesting. I don't ever recall getting a complaint or even hearing about a complaint from a non-conservative. For all the talk about the "liberal media," these people aren't satisfied with the fact they have Rush, Hannity, O'Reilly, Ingraham, Savage, Reagan, Dr. Laura, Glen Beck and on and on and on. Anyhow, my boss simply refers these big babies over to our talk station which is almost 100 percent conservative, and that's fine with me. All they seem to know how to do is scream "liberal!!!!" into the phone at me which I find funny since I consider myself a moderate. I think our political system has been broken for awhile now. I'm just not a conservative, and that seems to drive some people batty. I guess these guys all just temporarily went deaf for the eight years Clinton was in office. My God! We railed on him constantly!

INT: You did a thing on the air for awhile this summer called "Best Foot Forward" in which you attempted to point out to women in the audience what some of your attractive character traits are. Did it score you any babes?

JC: Well now, see? That's precisely why I stopped doing it. People thought I had sunk to using the station to troll for women.

INT: Weren't you?

JC: Yes. But I didn't want it to *look* that way!

INT: Ah-HA!!

JC: I was KIDDING. Seriously. Laurie Mac made an interesting point recently. She said, "JC, this act you're doing is great for ratings, but it's killing your social life." She's right, of course. What woman in her right mind would recommend me to an attractive, bright, available friend after listening to the over-the-top stuff we do on the show everyday? This goes back to what I was talking about earlier. The audience only knows as much as I want them to know. So I decided to talk on the air a little about some of my more endearing, human qualities because we thought people, women especially, were getting the wrong idea.

INT: And some of those qualities are…?

JC: Well, I throw my dirty clothes in the hamper at night instead of on the floor. I always get the car washed before I go out on a date. I always hold doors open for women.

INT: You're a real catch, aren't you?

JC: Fine. Be a smartass, but a very nice single mom e-mailed me to say she was teaching her teenage son a lot of the same things about how to treat a girl and that she really appreciated what I was saying.

INT: It's really important to you that women like you, isn't it?

JC: Yes. If a male listener doesn't like me I can handle it. If a woman listener, or even one of my female co-workers hates me, I'll go way out of my way to win her over.

INT: And why do you think you do that?

JC: Breasts, dummy.

INT: You like women, though. Right?

JC: I love 'em. But I also don't buy into all of this nonsense about "women: good; men: bad." Women will wear high heels to appear taller and panty hose to make their legs look smooth and sleek. They paint their nails, dye their hair, and apply a ton of makeup. They'll undergo breast augmentations, shoot Botox into their foreheads, and hang jewelry all over themselves and head out the door. Then they'll sit at the bar with their girlfriends and complain that "there just aren't any *real men* out there anymore."

INT: What's the oddest thing a woman has ever asked you?

JC: "Do these glasses make my ass look fat."

INT: Do you have a general philosophy about women?

JC: Someone once said, "Power is to women what cleavage is to men." If I could only get some.

INT: Power or cleavage?

JC: Hmmmm...

INT: Let's go back to the business side of things.

JC: GOOD!

INT: What do you wish you could change about your 20-year career in St. Louis broadcasting?

JC: I would have had more pictures taken when I had hair.

INT: And now the real answer...

JC: I can't seem to kill this idea some people have that I've been fired from every station in town.

INT: Because you haven't *worked* at every station in town?

JC: Hardy-har. You know what I mean. When I wrote the first book four years ago I went into great detail and even documented everything possible to prove that characterization of me is inaccurate. I even had published quotes from the newspapers and transcripts from broadcasts in which several of the general managers in question flat out said I wasn't fired and that there were other circumstances that led to my no longer working there.

INT: Ultimately, though, you were let go as opposed to still working there.

JC: Yes. But "fired"? As in: "You messed up. You did something wrong. Your ratings sucked?" No.

INT: Were you ever fired?

JC: Sure. But when people want to put a negative spin on my career and focus on how many stations I've worked at, I always like to point out I was also *hired* at all those stations, too. How many radio hosts could ever make that claim? At KSHE I just wore them out. There was so much controversy and legal hassle I think the company was simply exhausted and that led to an air of mistrust. The station was in the ionosphere ratings-wise, so when my contract was up after two-and-a-half years, they put something on the table they knew I'd never sign. Plus, I was 90 percent sure I was taking a job in Chicago, so we just walked away from one another. It wasn't until I decided to stay in St. Louis and took the job at KSD that things got ugly.

INT: What happened at KSD? You had a commanding first-place lead, the show couldn't have been bigger, yet you left there under a cloud of controversy in September of 1991.

JC: I'm not sure my lawyers are ever going to let me tell what really happened. I'd suggest going back and reading what they did let me say in my first book. The person who was responsible for breaking up the show, which eventually caused a ripple effect throughout the building resulting in lots of people losing their jobs and finally the sale of the station, would still love to sue the pants off me for telling the story. I won't give him the satisfaction.

INT: Even after all these years?

JC: Especially after all these years.

INT: Keep going...

JC: Well, I spent a year assembling a group to try and buy an FM station that was for sale. That was back in the days when you could get one for two or three million. We were just about to make our move when the FCC changed the ownership rules allowing companies to operate multiple properties. It shot the prices up tenfold and killed our chances. So I went to KMOX. I loved that move because nobody — and I mean *nobody* — saw it coming. It was sort of like my move over to K-HITS. All of the "experts" and wannabes on the Internet pretend to have some kind of inside track, and we all just laugh since some of these deals are in the works for months without anyone, oftentimes not even the people at the station I'm coming to, knowing anything. At this very moment, for example, my contract is expired with Emmis. I'm being courted by two different St. Louis radio stations, and almost nobody knows a thing about it.

INT: You were at KMOX for 53 shows. What happened?

JC: The short version is that it was over before it began. There was a five-week period between the announcement I was starting there and the date I actually went on the air, and in that time the station got eight hundred letters of protest. I read every one, by the way. Anyhow, the general manager of the station was so afraid of those old people who made up his base that he dropped all support of his own decision before I even did my first show, and I was left to hang. Fifty-three shows later it was over. I got the last laugh, though. All of those 800 people are dead now.

INT: From there you went to The River, right?

JC: Well, actually it was "The Fox" before it became "The River." A couple TV guys I'd known before picked up two weak-signaled FM stations. Before I signed with them they insisted they were about to move the broadcast tower from the extreme outskirts of the region to a site just north of Forest Park. We did reasonably well there, but after two years with listeners basically only being able to hear the station in their cars, the station brought in its third general manager in that two-year period — a mean and bizarre woman I couldn't work with. So when the contract expired I think both sides were fine with saying "buh-bye." Those guys who owned the place had shifted all of their time, energy, and money into launching that abysmal Channel 30 news operation anyhow, and the idea of having me and Trish Brown from KMOV and Mike Bush from KSDK as part of a morning show in their company suddenly became very, very un-cool. It wasn't until after the station moved that tower about a year after I left that The River finally was able to get on the map. The owners dumped all of their St. Louis properties, then took the money and ran. And do you want to hear something incredibly weird?

INT: Sure.

JC: That "mean, bizarre" woman I referred to at The River?

INT: Yeah...

JC: She married my ex-wife's creepy divorce lawyer!! Isn't it amazing how people like that just seem to find one another?

INT: When you went back for a second time to KSD you were hired by a woman who had once sued you for slander.

JC: Yes. Amazing what can happen when people get desperate enough, huh? That was a very bizarre and frustrating experience. There was a programmer running the soft rock station in the group that had the ear of the general manager who was fouling up everything our own program director was trying to accomplish. The station ended up getting sold three times in less than three years. For a period of a few months we actually weren't owned by *anyone*, and our paychecks were coming from a law firm in Boston. You know what? I'm getting sick to my stomach thinking about this. If anybody really wants to know any more about this, it's covered extensively in my first book. Next!

INT: Then you went to KTRS.

JC: Next...

INT: KLOU?

JC: Covered it in an earlier chapter. Why don't you have this conversation with Mark Klose? He's moved around more than me!

INT: You recently turned 50.

JC: You just had to, didn't you?

INT: Come on! That wasn't a shot! I'm trying to make a point.

JC: Go ahead. Go ahead...

INT: Well, you're 20 years older than you were when you arrived in town. How are you different?

JC: In most ways, I'm not. I'm still doing *this*. I'm just better at it. Health-wise, my doctor says I'm in better shape than almost anyone else he sees that's my age. I've had back trouble that led to two surgeries, and I've had surgery for a recurring problem with my left foot, and all of that keeps me from getting my gut down to a size I'd like, and it means I'm either in pain, or at least discomfort, a majority of the time. But I see huge fat guys 20 years younger than me who I'm in a lot better condition than. People I meet these days who don't know me are always almost 10 years off when they try to guess my age. A lot of that comes from good genes. My dad is pushing 83 and looks 70-something. But I never smoked, took drugs, or baked in the sun, either. I'm in a young person's business; most of my friends are quite a bit younger. I have two daughters under the age of twelve and for the last four years I've played shortstop every Monday night from April to October on a co-ed softball team made up of men and women in their twenties and thirties. That having been said, if you want to see someone in good shape, look at Ulett. He's 47, weighs under 155, and has almost zero body fat. Really pisses me off.

INT: Do you ever feel old?

JC: Never. Well, let me qualify that. When I see audiences laughing at Farrelly brothers movies, or when I see some of the 18-to-34 ratings on most of that crap called "reality TV," or when I see hordes of young women scarring their bodies for life with those horrible tattoos at the bottom of their backs I feel what I'd guess you'd call "culturally detached." Oh... can we stop for a moment? I have to chase some punks out of my yard.

INT: I got that. Okay. What about emotionally, personally?

JC: That's more complicated. I'm a little more open-minded than I was two decades ago which, I guess — which is the opposite of the way it is for most people. Politics, stupidity, and missed opportunity all still irritate me. I gave up on the pursuit of perfection a few years ago, and that's brought a lot more peace to me. And I try not to make any decisions when I'm mad anymore. That's made an enormous difference.

INT: You haven't mentioned anything about women.

JC: Am I supposed to?

INT: Well, anyone's who's listened to the show for five minutes can tell women factor into your life pretty significantly.

JC: I've been divorced for five years. We don't speak. And that's not by my doing. It really complicates things when you're trying to raise two kids. I've dated here and there, and I've been in and out of two relationships including one that ended a year ago that was off-and-mostly-on for three-and-a-half years.

INT: Do you see yourself getting married again?

JC: Didn't you just refer to me as a "great catch" a moment ago?

INT: Seriously.

JC: Yes. That's where I thought that last one was headed. I think I now understand I wasn't even close to being over the shock of the divorce along with the mind-boggling upheaval it brought to my personal life until just recently. I mean, for one thing, I went from being a family man with two kids living in a 14-room, 3800-square-foot home, to a single guy reduced to a tiny, two-bedroom condo. Now I understand something like that really messes you up in all sorts of ways you don't even understand until well afterwards. It doesn't matter what you do for a living, how much money you make, or what movie star you interviewed that morning. You come home to an empty place at night and it will f*** you up. Then I went out there to start dating and quickly had to accept the fact I didn't remember a thing about how to do it. Plus, even the younger women were older and much different than I remembered the last time I was single in the '80s. I made every conceivable mistake a newly single person could make.

INT: Translation: you hurt some people, didn't you?

JC: That I did.

INT: Blind dates? Set-ups? The Internet?

JC: The Internet thing scares me since everyone lies, though I did meet a lawyer that way I dated for about a year. I hadn't been on a blind date in over 20 years, but I went on three in one week recently. Mine aren't usually really "blind" anyway because they almost always know *me*. Then you have to deal with pre-conceived notions, and it's usually a mismatch because they think they're getting the guy on the radio. Anyhow, one produced a flash that burned out quickly, in another there was no chemistry, and the third I could write an entire book on it was such a nightmare. Incidentally, almost every single woman I know has a horror story about Internet dating. I'll bet you 80 percent of the guys women meet online are married or in a similar sort of relationship. On the upside, if you're looking to contract herpes I can't think of a better way.

INT: Let's shift back to the broadcasting business for a moment.

JC: GOOD!!

INT: You're not crazy about Madison Avenue's use of classic rock songs.

JC: I don't like the idea that these *teenagers* running the advertising world are reducing my generation's music to the level of zit cream commercial background music. Some of us hold a lot of that music in reverence. The most outrageous example occurred about a year ago when, I think it was a commercial for pants or something, used the first few lines of *Fortunate Son* by CCR in a real upbeat, sort of patriotic-themed spot. You know:

"Some folks are born made to wave the flag,
Oooh, they're red, white and blue."

That was a freakin' anti-war song, man! They totally subverted the meaning and spirit of the tune. John Fogerty would have been spinning in his grave except for the fact he's not dead yet!

INT: Do you consider yourself a cat person or a dog person?

JC: I guess you're only supposed to be one or the other, but I'm both. I had nothing but cats until the early '90s when we got Harry, a yellow Lab. We had to put him down four years ago, and I still miss him. My calico cat, Chloe, is 13, and I miss a little kitty named Sophia, too.

INT: What accounts for your intense love of baseball?

JC: The true answer sort of comes out in layers. On one hand, it's just such a perfect game. If Abner had placed those bases five feet further apart, the entire scope of the game would have been different. Somehow he knew ninety feet was the precise distance needed to produce the hundreds of bang-bang plays at first every year. It's also perfect for the masses. Unlike the experience of being a 12-foot football or basketball player, for example, nearly everyone has personally experienced the sensation of hitting, throwing, and catching a ball. For that reason, the game also connects us to our youth, and that's almost always a good thing.

INT: I agree. But those are reasons for everyone to like the game. What about you personally?

JC: Having an uncle playing for the Cubs when I was little and living in Chicago had a lot to do with it. The games being on WGN television and radio was also part of my early connections to broadcasting. As a player, pitching in championship games with a couple thousand people watching and stadium bunting and banners all over the place was probably an early introduction to "performing." And since my dad was always a coach or manager, I think baseball kept us connected during those rebellious years that can occur between a father and son. I still rebelled. Just not against him.

INT: That's not far from one of the main themes played out in one of your favorite movies, *Field of Dreams*.

JC: I guess I'm just realizing that now. But I'll tell you what else is so significant about baseball. It's amazing how the things I learned being a pitcher are all the same principles I still use today. Skeptics think those "Baseball is Life" t-shirts are corny, but it's true. The parallels are startling! Everyone's heard those oddities about a pitcher tossing a one-hitter and still losing the game, right? Well, that's like life. Sometimes you do *everything* right and still find yourself having lost. Also, during tournament play when I was competing in Babe Ruth League ball they had rules that prohibited the same kid from always being the starting pitcher. Instead, I'd have to be in the bullpen for some of the games, and I'd be the guy they'd bring in with the bases loaded and nobody out...and I just *loved* it!! I think I learned that if you know you're prepared it gives you the confidence to thrive in situations that would scare the hell out of most people. That's why I prepare, prepare, prepare even today.

INT: There's a lot of people who believe football has replaced baseball as the "national pastime."

JC: Yeah, well, when the NFL can prove they can get 30,000 to 40,000 fans in the stadium 162 nights a year instead of only 16, that's when I'll listen to them.

INT: The knock against you in the old days was that you were hostile to management and to the sales department. Was that a fair statement?

JC: Yes and no. Did I have a blanket policy of hostility toward them? I think it may have gotten that way after a long series of well-documented decisions affecting me made by specific managers and sales guys that most people in the business now recognize as having been suspect. I can tell you there's general resentment even today when a salesperson, for example, sets you up for an appearance at a business and doesn't follow through on details. Now *you're* the dope standing there while people are coming up asking all sorts of questions about giveaways and contests you can't answer. The sales guy has his commission, and you've got a bunch of people mad at *you*. Sometimes I wonder if I'm ever going to see the *respect* issue resolved between sales and programming.

INT: What about management?

JC: It's like a marriage. You try to hook up with someone you can respect, but you're still going to have disagreements, fights, and occasions when you wish you were dead. That having been said, at this place and the last place I worked I've had a great relationship with my immediate supervisors. They've really helped me which is what they're there for, not to be tough guys or to throw up roadblocks all over the place.

INT: You've never seemed afraid to go after certain public figures on the show. Do you have a general set of rules about that?

JC: I don't go "looking" for people to rip on. A person has to sort of be asking for it, or they must have distinguished themselves in some kind of public fashion that clashes with my beliefs or the general laws of nature. It gets a little murky on occasion because I try to avoid kicking someone when they're down. Then you get a situation like the Mike Danton/Katie Wolfmeyer story, and you simply have no choice. As tragic as it is for the people and their families, I have to take it on or I'm not doing my job.

INT: You spend a lot of time on *The Showgram* talking about movies, and you've been known to see well over a hundred films a year. Do you believe "critics," per se, have any effect on what people see or don't see?

JC: I think there's a small, loyal percentage of very active filmgoers who pay a lot of attention to their favorite critics and will often base their decisions on what Ebert and Roeper say, for example. The average American sees about a half dozen movies a year at the theater and makes his or her decisions based on individual personal taste or affinity for a particular movie star. There's another whole group that goes along with a general buzz or ends up at a movie because of a group decision. Where a critic's recommendations can come into play is when someone plans an evening around a movie, gets the babysitter, has a nice dinner, and shows up at the theater only to find the movie they'd planned to see sold out. Now they're standing there staring at the other 19 titles on the board trying to make a decision. In that situation, someone might say, "Hey...I heard J.C say *The House of Sand and Fog* was good." That's where I think I might serve some purpose. What's really pathetic is there's not another city this size in the country that doesn't have at least one TV station with a full-time entertainment person doing movie stuff. Something like 30,000 people will see a movie on a typical weekend in St. Louis. I can think of dozens of events and activities our local stations cover that don't draw anywhere near that number, yet they've copped this attitude about movie coverage. It doesn't make any sense.

INT: What about those quotes in the movie ads in the paper?

JC: If you knew what a corrupt, dirty racket that is and just who those guys are you'd never even ask again. They're called "quote whores." That should tell you a lot.

INT: You've broadcast from the Abbey Road Studios in London, and you play four Beatles songs each morning on your "Fab Four" feature. What's at the heart of all that?

JC: I never thought my generation would get over the loss of John Lennon. Then, after a very long hiatus, Paul started doing Beatles songs at concerts mixed in with his other music, and he and the other surviving members talked a lot about the genuine love they had for one another. It seemed to help everyone get over what had happened. But when George died, I was crushed. I can't exactly put my finger on it, but I still feel very bad about it. He seemed so quiet and unassuming that people were often surprised by his wit but never by his wisdom. This is the guy who wrote *My Sweet Lord*, but in *Taxman* he also wrote: "...if you take a walk I'll tax your feet." His passing is so very sad and at the same time invigorating knowing how spiritual he was and that he was so at peace with the idea of moving onto the next world. Having said all that, the "Fab Four" feature is really there primarily because I like their music, and I know our core listeners do, too.

INT: Harrison was a Hindu, and a big part of what Hindus believe is that you should be somewhat dedicated to pursuing the meaning of life. Wanna take a swipe at that?

JC: Think of how often you'll recall something that happened when you were only nine or ten years old. Something so insignificant at the time that the person who it involved couldn't possibly have been expected to know the kind of impact it would have on you. Now think about how much time we spend trying to influence the people around us. We teach our kids everything we know. We sit around and tell stories, some funny, some serious, to our friends. We used to take photographs of everything important. Now we videotape everything from a baby's first step to a parent's retirement party. And what's left when we leave the earth?

INT: Those photos and videos.

JC: And the *memories*. That's it. That's what I believe the meaning and purpose of life is. To leave memories. It's the only thing that makes any sense to me.

INT: Pretty heavy.

JC: Yeah, well, you asked. Besides, I think you become sort of introspective when you spend an entire spring and summer writing a book. Plus it's been a very, very weird and stressful year. Some people drink or do drugs, some people turn to religion, some people crumble...I wrote a book.

INT: What do you think you'll be doing in ten years?

JC: From the looks of things, still talking to you.

INT: And now the real answer...

JC: Well, I know I have to either quit this job or get fired.

INT: Why would you even say something like that?

JC: I have to. I want to be the only person in the history of St. Louis radio to take four separate "also-ran" morning shows from the bottom to number one.

INT: (pause) Somehow that's both disturbing and admirable at the same time.

JC: Thank you.

INT: Anything else you want to do?

JC: I'd like Michael Feldman's job on *Whad'ya Know?* And when my daughters get a little older I'd still like to do some more work in a TV newsroom.

INT: Doing entertainment and movie reviews again?

JC: Maybe. I think it's absolutely pathetic that this is one of the only local television markets I know of that doesn't have anyone doing legitimate, full-time movie and entertainment stuff. But actually I'd like a stab at that weather gig.

INT: After all the criticisms you've had of those people?!

JC: Well, all the TV manager-types in St. Louis are still caught up on the whole "meteorologist" thing. It's not like that in other cities. There's lots of people doing weather who aren't meteorologists, but they have compelling or entertaining personalities that make viewers want to watch them. We know meteorologists are full of it anyhow. They won't cop to the fact that they can't really predict weather more than a day or two in advance in most cases. I'd like to do weather in a way that it hasn't been done here before.

INT: Let's end on something upbeat. Do you have a favorite joke?

JC: Yes. Did you hear about the Catholic escaped convict who gave himself up for Lent?

INT: No. What happened?

JC: No... that's the joke.

INT: (long pause) Ohhhhhhhh, I get it.

JC: Hmmm. But how did you get this job?

INT: Thanks. We're done.

JC: We're never done.

Chapter 18

"The rats keep winning the rat race."
"I'm Not Gonna Let It
Bother Me Tonight"
Atlanta Rhythm Section

If we're lucky, by the time this book hits the newsstands our beloved St. Louis Cardinals may again be basking in the glory of another World Series championship. "The one constant, Ray, is baseball." That was one of the pivotal lines in W. P. Kinsella's *Field of Dreams*. And it seems *Baseball in St. Lou* has taught us several important lessons of late.

The meteoric rise of Albert Pujols proves that, sometimes, nice guys can finish first. The passing of Darryl Kile reminds us that's not always true. Though nobody gave them any kind of a chance in the preseason, the Cardinals' record-breaking year in 2004 taught us not to believe or necessarily accept everything we hear. The imminent destruction of Busch Stadium is a reminder that all things must pass and that the world is in a constant state of change.

In the midst of the Redbirds' quest for the title in October of 1996, Becky Povich of St. Peters was one of a dozen or so listeners to call in to our show during a segment in which we asked fans to relate their favorite Cardinals memory. It turned out she'd actually given birth to her first son, Mark, at DePaul Hospital right in the middle of the Cardinals' World Series with Minnesota in 1987. She recalled the nursing staff sticking cardboard signs and logos on the basinets of the newborns. Now her son was nine years old and somewhat disappointed his mom, the real baseball fan in the family, had been unsuccessful at scoring playoff tickets for St. Louis' league championship series with the Atlanta Braves.

What Becky didn't know was that she was participating in a contest. We had decided to present a pair of primo tickets for that night's game to the caller we felt told the most compelling story of Cardinals fandom. We almost lost her when she was informed what was going on. KMOV's Laurie Waters happened to hear the whole thing transpiring on the air, and when Becky showed up at the station later that morning, cameras were rolling as she claimed her tickets. Becky's husband, Ron, was generous enough to settle for a TV dinner and the game on the tube while his wife and their son watched the game from the tenth row field boxes behind the Cards dugout.

We give prizes away on the show all the time. This was different. This day I made a friend. I'm happy to say Becky and I speak frequently and Mark, now seventeen, is still a big time Cardinals fan.

The great Lou Brock once said, "When all you can talk about is what you used to do, it's time to go." Well, we won't be going anytime soon. The energy we get from knowing we're still getting it done for the St. Louis radio audience will drive *The Showgram* for as long as you still want us. We're all older now, and that's not always a good thing in such a youthful business. But in the long run, age and guile usually beat youth and enthusiasm. Besides, failure isn't nearly as frightening as regret and unrealized potential.

Sometimes I think about how my entire life and career might have been changed had only one or two things along the way turned out differently. Had the hideous turn of events that led to the end of our KSD show in 1991 played out another way, the entire FM dial might look completely different now. Had KMOX actually given me a fair chance in 1993 that whole station might sound different today. Had television stations in Fort Wayne and Omaha gone through with plans to hire me, I might not have continued on in radio or even gotten to St. Louis. But that would have meant we wouldn't have had all this.

I'm much more inclined these days to let the rats win the rat race. I've replaced an obsession with radio wars, trivialities, and pissing matches with things of a higher mind. At the University of Pennsylvania in May of 2004, U2's Bono delivered the commencement address. Here's one small part of his message that day:

> "If you want to serve the age, betray it. Betraying the age means exposing its conceits, its foibles, its phony moral certitudes. It means telling the secrets of age and facing harsher truths. Every age has its massive, moral blind spots."

There are plenty of shows that will make you laugh occasionally. We want to make you think, too. I'll take my chances on that being the right decision. We may insult you periodically, but we'll try never to insult your intelligence.

Thank you for everything. I wouldn't trade the past 20 years in St. Louis for the world.

Biography

One of St. Louis' most recognizable people, J.C. Corcoran is a successful radio and television personality, author and father. Upon his arrival in the Gateway City, J.C. was officially named "God's Gift to Radio," a title he still holds today.

It's hard to name a celebrity J.C. hasn't interviewed or a topic to which he hasn't added his unique perspective. For variety, Corcoran has taken his show on the road from Chicago (for various Cards-Cubs weekends and from the first-ever night game at Wrigley Field), Phoenix (from the first game of the departed "Big Red," now known as the Phoenix Cardinals), Milwaukee (in the thick of the 1998 Mark McGwire record-setting home run season), Hawaii, Jamaica, the Bahamas, San Francisco, Mexico, Minneapolis, Kansas City, Disney World, the "Rock and Roll Hall of Fame" in Cleveland, the "Grammys" in both New York and L.A., and from high above St. Louis in the Blockbuster Video blimp. Corcoran's series of live broadcasts in 1989 from the Abbey Road Studios in London will long be remembered. And in 1990 "J.C. and The Breakfast Club" became the first morning show to emanate entirely from Moscow.

But on any typical morning you'd be just as likely to hear J.C. talking about what's going on in St. Louis. In addition, there's hardly a single, charitable organization that hasn't directly benefited from exposure on J.C.'s radio show, including The Salvation Army, for whom he's personally helped raise nearly a quarter-million dollars and over fifty tons of food via "The Food and Cash Salvation Bash" and "The Cans Film Festival."

It was during his stint at KLOU in 2001 when he was honored by "The St. Louis Air Awards" with the prestigious March of Dimes "Lifetime Achievement Award."

In addition to his radio work, J.C. spent seven years as Entertainment

Editor for KMOV-TV, St. Louis' CBS television affiliate. His celebrity interviews, movie reviews and live reports from major entertainment events, concerts and comedy clubs were a fixture on local television from 1985, when he performed the same function at KSDK-TV(NBC), through 1998. During that period, J.C. made roughly three hundred trips to New York and Los Angeles to gather material.

Corcoran won an Emmy for his 1990 half-hour special entitled, "J.C. Went to Cardinals Spring Training and All We Got Was This Lousy TV Show." In 1989 he was a featured guest on a spirited edition of the "Sally Jessy Raphael Show" that dealt with music censorship.

In 1998, Corcoran was notified that his annual "home opener" baseball special was added to the archives at the Major League Baseball Hall of Fame in Cooperstown, New York.

J.C. lives in St. Louis County with his cat, Chloe, four satellite TV receivers, six VCRs and three TiVos. Young girls have been seen entering and exiting his home at all hours, most notably his two daughters, Addison, 11, and Whitney, 9.

J.C. can be reached at www.jcontheline.com.